New Architecture San Francisco

New
Architecture
San
Francisco

Text by James Shay, A.I.A.
Photographs by Christopher Irion
Introduction by Sally B. Woodbridge

Chronicle Books • San Francisco

Acknowledgments

☐ We want to thank all the architects who, through their work, made this book possible. We greatly appreciate the generous giving of their time. We also wish to express our thanks to all the owners of the projects included here who allowed us to photograph their buildings.

Although not listed on the cover, the third creator of this book is Tom Ingalls, who brought us to Chronicle Books, and who, with his associate Gail Grant, provided the design. They designed the beautiful format, cover, and page layouts which contain our own work.

David Barich and Annie Barrows of Chronicle Books assisted us at Chronicle Books and provided timely and efficient handling of our work.

Our editor, Deborah Stone, made these talks about architecture intelligible when they wandered into the arcane.

We greatly appreciate Sally Woodbridge's introduction. Her insightful and knowledgeable comments about the discussion and presentation of architecture will serve the reader well.

Photographer's assistant Craig McDonald assisted in much of the photography. Without his competent support many of these photographs would not have been possible.

Susan Lockwood performed the mammoth task of transcribing almost 400 pages of recorded interviews. Her persistence in the face of recordings made in restaurants and other loud environs, as well as in conference rooms, saved many remarks and thoughts from oblivion.

We want to thank Bill Leddy for reading and commenting on many of these interviews as they were done. We valued his thoughtful remarks, and used them as guides throughout the interviews.

As the work required to produce the photographs and interviews increased, the support of our wives, Martha and Karen, respectively, helped us finish what had become an enormous undertaking. We greatly appreciate their assistance and encouragement.

A number of these photographs were previously published in *Architectural Record, Architecture, Restaurant and Hotel Design*, and *House Beautiful*. The photos of the Spencer House, by William Turnbull, appear courtesy of Hearst publications.

—Christopher Irion and James Shay

Printed in Japan.

Library of Congress Cataloging-in-Publication Data
Shay, James.
     New architecture San Francisco / text by James Shay; photographs by Christopher Irion.
         p.   cm.
     ISBN 0-87701-537-6
     1. Architecture—California—San Francisco. 2. Architecture, Modern—20th century—California—San Francisco. 3. Architects—California—San Francisco—Interviews. 4. San Francisco (California)—Buildings, structures, etc. I. Irion, Christopher. II. Title.
NA735.S35S53   1989
720'.9794'61—dc20   89-35466
                                                                          CIP

ISBN: 0-87701-537-6
Editing: Deborah Stone
Book and cover design: Ingalls + Associates, San Francisco
Designers: Gail Grant, Thomas Ingalls
Composition: Wilsted & Taylor Publishing Services

Distributed in Canada by:
Raincoast Books
112 East Third Avenue
Vancouver B.C.
V5T 1C8

10 9 8 7 6 5 4 3 2 1

Chronicle Books
275 Fifth Street
San Francisco, California 94103

Table of Contents

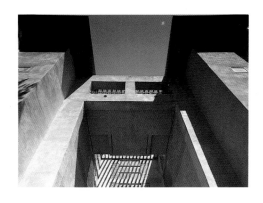

Introduction

☐ Architects used to be content to speak through their works. Indeed, architects have so identified with form that they have had no difficulty asking buildings to speak for them. The revered modern master Louis Kahn was famous for his query, "What does the building want to be?" instead of, "What do I want the building to be?" This tradition of anthropomorphizing architecture continues—in his interview in these pages William Turnbull says, "If you site the building right, it's going to feel like it's been there for a while." But increasingly, the public is hearing directly from architects, generally in the interview format used by James Shay for this book.

Much of architects' talk is about their ideas and the frustrations of expressing them in their buildings. Although they are supposed to practice the discipline they have spent many years in school learning, architects are increasingly called upon to react, like politicians, to the vagaries of complex and seemingly unending processes that have little to do with the corpus of learning from which they derive their expertise. Many more people are now involved in the building process: not just the clients, who are often multiple, but the neighbors, the community planners, design review boards, preservation activists—all of whom seem bent on savaging the architect's intentions.

The perception that buildings now have more to do with the will of outsiders than with the architects' ideas has intensified a longstanding interest in unbuilt designs for buildings. Architects now preserve more of their early sketches for projects large and small, partially in the hope of salvaging a record of their ideas from the ravages of process. This introspection has also produced a nostalgia for the hypothetical good old days when architects did not have to be politicians or bureaucrats or spokesmen, but could simply sit in their offices and do what they have been trained to do: play creatively with forms in space. The reader will find suggestions in these interviews that there is almost nothing left of architecture. Whatever it is that is out there may be interesting or fun or profitable for a lot of people, but architecture it isn't. But in spite of their frustrations, few architects would deny that both they and their works are enjoying an unprecedented amount of attention from the public. (Indeed, this book would not have found a publisher less than a decade ago.) If this interest leads to more consequential recognition, we may all be better off.

Readers new to the internal culture of architecture may be amazed at its blatant narcissism and the dependency on cross-referencing past architects and movements little known outside the field. But if architects have a deep need to validate their work through grounding it in the past, they also derive strength from jumping up and down on the graves of their ancestors. So,

along with the need for roots and connections goes a hairshirt impulse toward purges. Mark Mack observes that, "We used Laugier as a kind of cleansing agent." The idea of Laugier, a seventeenth-century cleric and eminent theoretician, in a can is arresting. But far from trivializing this eminent prophet of austerity, Mack is expressing kinship with him.

We may find architects' verbal description of the intentions behind a given design informative or incredible, depending on our mood. Knowing that the Oakland office building called Leviathan, designed by Ace Architects partly for their own use, is the embodiment of a hair-raising sci-fi vision of the building in the eternal embrace of an undersea monster may well inspire us to visit it. Disappointed that the vision isn't literal, we may then wonder what moved the architects to torture their quite reasonable design with such imagery.

If some architects need flights of fancy to sustain their craft, others express a rocklike faith in materials and, as Hanns Kainz put it, the basic elements of architecture: the door, the window, the stairs, the column. Perhaps Kainz emphasized these elements, because others, such as the walls and the roof, are often the main carriers of style. In any case, his selection reveals an attitude toward these compositional elements that has concerned architects since Vitruvius. Kainz confronts himself in the challenge of designing a stair that will not repeat his previous efforts. Here the architect is doing something that enlists training and talent in ways that are crucial to the continuation of architecture, never mind how the result is described in words.

Architects seem to be both enamored and mistrustful of words. Peter Pfau and Wes Jones state in their interview that, "We try hard not to talk about architectural things with the normal language that we were all trained to talk about it with—it has a lot to do with not limiting the results. In the studio, which is where everything happens, we communicate . . . in much more of a coded language . . . saying things like 'couldn't you just tweak that a little, or add more flipper over here?'" Yet, architectural jargon is no more arcane than that of any other occupation; its function in architecture as elsewhere is to separate the insiders from the outsiders and to instill confidence and a sense of intimacy on the part of the insiders with the work at hand. Since words are not their primary materials, architects are not likely to use them judiciously. But they are less likely to strain for hype than the writers who promote their works in the press and in brochures where we may read that a given design is therapeutic, but not pharmaceutical, that spaces are neutral without being servile, and stuff like that.

Architects are trained to question, to metaphorically reinvent the wheel. This is the creative part of what they do, and, for that reason, they recoil from the idea of designing in a style if that implies, as it often does, simply following rules. *Bending* rules is something else; architects view this exercise as an opportunity both to innovate and to comment on the state of their art. No matter how much architects decry style as the commodification of architecture, it is arguably one of architecture's most easily communicated and therefore successfully marketed aspects. Although some readers may wonder why all the fuss in these interviews about the pros and cons of modernism and postmodernism, the two terms have wide public recognition largely because they refer, albeit imprecisely, to styles. Although Shay has wisely provided a glossary of terms, concise definitions that are also inclusive are probably out of the question.

Lately, even regionalism which, in the last turning of the wheel of fashion, was a return to the basics of climate and topography with an admixture of local cultural attitudes, is now considered a style. Some architects feel obliged to disengage themselves from it. Contextualism is also tainted with style since in many instances the styles of the buildings that make up the context of a new design are seen as an unwelcome determinant. Yet, designers for city-scale projects disagree. Dan Solomon believes that one of the strengths of his firm's infill housing projects in San Francisco is its stylistic responsiveness to neighborhood and even citywide typologies. Skidmore Owings and Merrill architects Mark Goldstein and John Kriken see the use of urban patterns not as stylistic preservation but as a means of creating images that people can test against their own values. Certainly, for many of the architects interviewed here, the Bay region's special qualities have been a most profound inspiration.

One theme that weaves its way through the interviews with interesting variations is the attitude of architects toward clients, often called by the more sociological term "users." Some of the architects probe their clients' hearts and minds at length in an effort to, as William Turnbull puts it, "smoke out their dreams and desires." For Turnbull's former partner Donlyn Lyndon, the process is more like a playful exercise that involves not giving the clients their first expectation. "We would like architecture to be that we're providing things they (the clients) didn't expect, and that they're connecting with them and making things out of them that we don't expect."

In the case of speculative projects which do not have real clients, architects often nominate themselves as prospective users. Or, they may consider the place, the community, or the landscape as the ultimate client. Their experience working with the complexities of the urban context lead Solomon, Goldstein and Kriken to speak about broader responsibilities to city form and the environment.

Few architects speak about environmental and social imperatives; fewer still discuss the nuts and bolts of getting their projects built. (The firm of Fisher-Friedman is a notable exception to the last.) Whether or not the architects' creative process is the most interesting aspect of their practice, it is definitely a subject that architects don't feel has been adequately covered. Unlike practitioners of the so-called fine arts, architects cannot fully realize their ideas in the studio. Increased recognition of the value of architects' drawings as works of art may offer some compensation for their never achieving three-dimensional form, but in the final analysis, architecture is incomplete without users. We the public only really comprehend architecture when we experience it fully by walking around and through it. Even photographs, one of the most common ways of seeing architecture, are edited versions of buildings taken from points of view selected by the photographer, possibly with the architect's help but often without it. The challenge is to convey a three-dimensional medium in a framed, two-dimensional one. The photographer must use his eye to compose the image of the subject so that the viewers' eyes will move over it easily as if the real thing were before them. Fortunately, in this book James Shay's interviews are balanced with Christopher Irion's exemplary photographs of the interviewees' projects; the combination offers an illuminating armchair tour of the intentions of architecture.

Sally B. Woodbridge

Foreword

☐ This is a book about architecture in the architects' words and images. We think this kind of book, which we have always preferred over other books about architecture, is important today for two reasons. First of all, a consequence of the emergence of architecture in the 70s and 80s as a popular art form is a cultural view that often locates architecture somewhere between advertisements for designer jeans and arcane philosophy. Newsracks and bookstores are full of the very latest pronouncements from editors on what's hot and what's not, and why it's important to know that today's leading "ism" is about to be bumped-off by the latest, just-discovered "neo-whatever." What we, as architects, really do, why we do it, and its value is often drowned out by the braying of editors. Very seldom is there good writing about such diverse aspects of the life of an architect as the architect-client relationship, or how we design, or the personal rewards and frustrations of a life in architecture.

Second, the decades of the 70s and 80s in architecture had an unusual vitality because of the questioning that went on about modernism, the century's dominant architectural attitude. There has been, and continues to be, much debate in the profession about new directions. We wanted to talk about where architecture has been and where it's going with its day-to-day practitioners.

This book presents a variety of architecture. When the work of a particular area is written about in the architectural press there sometimes is a tendency to group together architects that seem to share philosophical affinities and stylistic similarities and present them in such a way that they come to stand for an area or region. For example, when we think of the contemporary architecture of Los Angeles in the 80s we inevitably think of Frank Gehry, B.A.M., and Frederick Fisher, as well as Mayne and Rotundi and Erik Moss. Yet there are many good architects in Los Angeles doing work that bears little relation to theirs, and which is seldom published, because it isn't a certain kind of hip modernist architecture. When work from the Bay Area is written about, or museum and gallery shows of the work are mounted, it is often Bay Area regionalist work. There is a great deal of excellent regionalist work done in the area, and the area's rich tradition is important and worth preserving, but a very high level of passion, care, and thought goes into creating equally important architecture in many different manners in the Bay Area. We believe that these diverse attitudes deserve recognition, attention, and study.

We began this project with a list of sixteen firms and individuals that reoccurred in discussion with editors, critics, and other architectural professionals as representing a cross section of work being done in and around San Francisco.

This grew to twenty-two, and finally, to over thirty. The names included represent work being done of all scales, from bathroom remodels to city planning. There are many fine individuals and firms doing equally outstanding work beyond those here, which we were unable to include because of space constraints. We regret that Joseph Esherick chose not to participate.

Each transcribed interview ran from eight to twenty-seven single-spaced typed pages. These were edited to two to five pages, with great emphasis during the editing on allowing the speaker's original thoughts and voice to remain intact. An attempt was made to have each interviewee review the edited transcript and make minor modifications related to clarification.

Although very few architects do not love to theorize, it is difficult for many of us who design, draw, build, and photograph buildings to, in William Turnbull's words, create "word constructs" about why we do what we do and why it has value. The day-to-day practice of architecture does not permit the luxury of sustained reflection and thought about one's own work. Nevertheless, in the course of most interviews there emerged a thoughtful kind of expressiveness that began to explain actions. These expressions ranged from Robert Overstreet's personal remarks about his education, to Peter Pfau and Wes Jones's detailed explanation of where they stand with regard to a particular type of architectural theory. Almost always each individual or firm we interviewed was able to present a clear picture of why they do what they do. We hope the reader will find these words, and the drawings and images, as interesting as we have.

Christopher Irion and James Shay

New Architecture San Francisco

Ace Architects

Lucia Howard and David Weingarten

From its office in Oakland's Hieroglyph Building, the firm of Ace Architects pursues what they call literal, as opposed to abstract, architecture. Lucia Howard and David Weingarten, 1978 graduates of the University of California at Berkeley, head the firm, which will soon be moving to its new office building being designed for a site near the Oakland waterfront. Ace Architects has received diverse honors, including awards from the Architectural League and the Graham Foundation for Advanced Studies in the Fine Arts. Recently, they were among "40 under 40," an exhibit of young architects curated by Philip Johnson and Robert Stern with Andrew MacNair.

JS: What is "egghead postmodernism"?

AA: "Egghead postmodernism" is a term coined by the architecture critic of the *San Francisco Chronicle*, Allan Temko, to describe the building we designed on Shattuck Avenue in Berkeley. I think he means that we overthink our designs and their relationships to other buildings. He thinks, I suspect, that the relationships between buildings ought to be contained in similarities rather than in oppositions.

One of the things architecture can do is to provoke visceral responses. There is some truth to the idea that too much content in a building is, to use his phrase, too egghead, but I don't think he's right in accusing us of that. A lot of new building is abstract and difficult to really get a hold of. We're more interested in buildings that make their contents known. Though we try to make buildings whose ideas are obvious and accessible, we think there is also room for more intellectual buildings.

JS: Well, only intellectual in a certain way. Your buildings are quite intellectual. I think you're equating intellectual with being abstract.

AA: It also means remote.

The article about us was a funny thing. Temko talked about the Shattuck Building and the library down the street to which it refers, saying that the library was the butt of a joke in our design, which is all wrong. I love the library. He thinks that because we attempt to make some connection between our building and another one nearby that we're making a joke about the other building. That misses the point of what we're trying to do, which in that case is to relate the building to its specific place in the world.

As far as being postmodern goes. . . . Ace is called postmodern by some, but that's not what we claim to be, unless it infuriates certain people, I suppose, like architecture critics.

JS: The building is quite notorious.

AA: The time when the building was being completed was a remarkable time around the

office because we received all sorts of anonymous phone calls, many advising us to give up architecture. Very, very rude calls, and all sorts of letters. It was quite a summer. We also received supportive calls from people who knew our work and thought the buildings were wonderful. Friends, clients, and even people we didn't know at all called to tell us not to be discouraged and to tell us stories of artists whose work wasn't appreciated in their time.

JS: Yet, many of your designs tend to be a bit shocking. Aren't you stirring the pot? Does shock value ever enter your thoughts when you design?

AA: Yes, I think it does. Locating a building is not simply a matter of making things blend in

Left: Shattuck Avenue Building, Berkeley.

Top right: Shattuck Avenue Building, Berkeley. Bottom right: Shattuck Avenue Building; detail.

but also a way of relating things to their places in ways that are unexpected. That's where buildings have shock value. If the Shattuck Building were on Melrose Avenue in L.A., no one would blink an eye.

JS: On Melrose it would be just another showroom.

AA: Right. But, up here, because of its radical juxtaposition to the other buildings on Shattuck Avenue it is shocking. Juxtaposition, though, may be seen as point and counterpoint, a relation of opposites.

JS: Or that there is no black without white.

AA: Exactly. And I also think that we both believe that while there are many good things in Bay Area architecture, it nonetheless can use a little shaking up or a little rattling from time to time.

We have arrived at this view through the response to our own work, such as the building on Lakeshore Avenue in Oakland. Everybody loves that building but thinks it's a remodel, which it isn't. It's a new building. People like Don Lyndon, who is really a very smart guy, asked me, "Was that just a remodeling of an existing building?" And, of course it wasn't. It was a brand new building that was very close to a 20s or 30s Spanish Revival.

JS: I've seen it from the freeway, which is the best place to see it. I always thought it was a remodel.

AA: Our next project was Shattuck. We thought at the time that our new work was a little bit on the wrong track, because of the Lakeshore building. We didn't want our new work looking like remodels. It's extremely important to be able to do new work in architecture. That's getting harder and harder to do, especially in the Bay Area.

JS: I know. Finding the land is harder and harder. And there are now infinite reviews and approvals for everything.

AA: Yes. Each of us, as architects, get only a certain number of chances. So, given that, we prefer to err on the side of excess and overcooking the pot.

JS: You mentioned that the Shattuck Building appropriates pieces from both the nearby Berkeley Public Library and the UC Berkeley campus visible in the distance. For the record, what are these appropriations?

AA: From the library there is the basic kind of decorative organization. That building, which is a big 30s Mayan job, or something, is a big block, with pilasters and capitals on the corners done in applied relief. Those are solid elements. Between them are openings—windows—that have peaked, chevron-shaped tops. That is on our building, in the corners. And then, as you come up Allston Way, perpendicular to Shattuck, a transparent, metal mesh tower prefigures the university campanile in the distance.

The snakes crawling over the parapets are our

version of the little creatures at the top of the windows on the library, which are snakish, sea horsish creatures that appear to pull up the points of the library's chevron windows.

JS: Well, that's a wild idea. I want to talk with you about the new office building you're designing for Oakland, which will include space for your own offices. What are the design concepts in the building?

AA: The building is made up of three parts, all related to structures you might find down by the Embarcadero and the port. The rear portion is like the part of a supertanker that contains the bridge and will be in deeply corrugated material. Then, there is a checkerboard pattern created with the windows, like the red and white checkerboards you see on buildings to identify

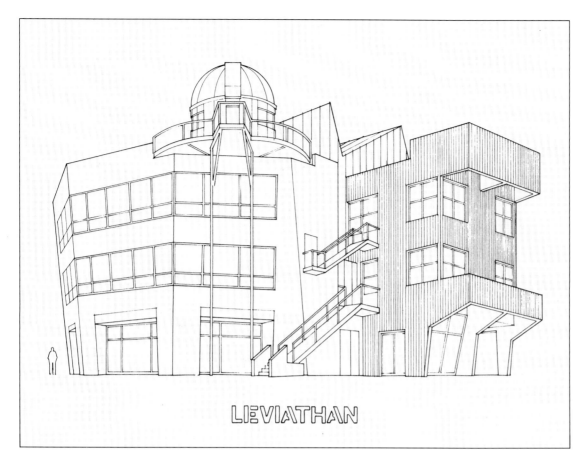

LEVIATHAN

Left: office building, Oakland.

Below: Darrell Place Condominiums, San Francisco. The columns in each corner of the room form an aedicula.

them as hazards, like at airports or on tanks—that sort of thing. That's the rear portion of the building. The front portion will be blue-green with walls canting out over the sidewalk. This will be like the control towers in airports, the buildings that contain people observing and controlling what is going on before them.

JS: Why is that important?

AA: First of all, it's another kind of building form that you find by the Embarcadero. For example, it is the typical shape for the cab of a crane or the bridge of a ship. Where the blue-green part comes to a point, it leans out like the bow of a great ship. Crawling over the top of this is a great sea monster, depicted in the forms of the sawtooth skylights.

JS: You are literally thinking of that as an abstracted sea monster?

AA: Right, as if it crawled out of the estuary and onto the top of the building. The creature's head and beak jut out at the corner as it struggles to overcome the taut-skinned structure rising from the street. A rotating observatory dome crowns the head, housing the creature's brain—in reality to be the partners' office. It will be done in a silvery kind of galvanized metal. The last parts, the supports under the beak, are thought of as the tentacles of the monster.

JS: Why do you have sea monsters crawling on the tops of your buildings?

AA: Well, it's contextual.

JS: I have heard many people claim to be profound contextualists. Please explain.

AA: Well, of course, contextualism is an overused word, which is why, as a word, it has great appeal. This building is one that we hope will make its subjects apparent. That is why we have the literal renditions of different kinds of building within this building.

We are trying to do something I think is difficult, because the context, for us, includes more than the setting. For many people what contextual means is that you paint the building a kind of beige or dark brown and put it behind some trees, so that it goes away. We're more interested in the idiosyncratic and peculiar relationships than in the ones where you put a trellis over everything. It will probably sound like heresy coming from Ace Architects, but we think there are some rich things in the modern tradition. We think of the modern idiom as one tradition we can use. It's like arts and crafts, neoclassical, or Spanish colonial revival. It's one of the ways in which you can build. This building is very modern for us, but that's because its context is so modern. Oakland is the greatest shipping terminus on the West Coast outside of Los Angeles and it's full of great cranes and container ships. We admire modernism and the strength and completeness of its vision. We find it appropriate for this building. I think where it fails us is that as a discipline we find it too subtle. We're not subtle. We're convinced that in a contemporary world people don't notice subtle

modernist work, so that it doesn't enter their lives in any particular way. It doesn't engage people at all. What we're really trying to do is just coax our work up to the level of consciousness at which people can interact with it.

In addition to this, the sea monster comes from a specific recollection of a 60s science fiction movie called, I think, *It Came from Beneath the Sea*.

JS: The building is in part a remembrance of the movie *It Came from Beneath the Sea*?

AA: Yeah, it's a science fiction movie I saw when I was a child and haven't seen since. One of the best parts of the movie was the octopus-squid sort of thing, very large, making various stops on its tour around the world, causing scenes of havoc. One of its stops is San Francisco. It never gets out of the water. All it does is use its tentacles to grab things. It grabs the Ferry Building and destroys it, and it grabs downtown and crumbles it.

JS: So, that is a, I guess we could call it, contextual memory.

AA: Yes, and the other part of the memory is again a movie, that of Captain Nemo and his Nautilus submarine.

JS: In contrast to the way you designed the office building, I believe you designed your two-unit building on Darrell Place in San Francisco as an exposition of the periods of Bay regionalist architecture.

AA: Yes. According to historians, the first Bay regional style is Bernard Maybeck, Willis Polk, and Ernest Coxhead. The second is William Wurster and similar architects, and the third is Charles Moore and those guys. What we did on that project was, on a very small lot, try to construct an archeology of the Bay region style. Each style is represented by characteristic elements from the period, so that, for example, in the first Bay region period the references are to English late eighteenth- and early nineteenth-century architecture: Willis Polk, Bernard Maybeck. The second period is a kind of international style, such as that practiced by Gardner Dailey. And the third period is represented by the aedicula-like job that plunges down through the upper unit.

We made the project an archeology, a reconstruction, because it's on Telegraph Hill, one of the oldest areas of town. The site is in a gulch, so that during the fire following the earthquake it wasn't hit. There is a whole range of quite early buildings up there, some pretty nice things. We wanted to respect them and to recognize the historic site. At the same time we wanted to make a building that extends the series of Bay region styles into a fourth and current period.

Above and right: Darrell Place Condominiums, San Francisco.

Amick Harrison

Lynn Harrison

Above: Kiiroihana Restaurant, San Francisco.

Amick Harrison was established in 1979 in San Francisco. The firm designs a variety of commercial and residential projects as well as interior tenant work throughout the Bay Area. Completed work ranges in scale from interior residential work to midrise office buildings and large scale planned unit developments. Among their recent projects are the handsome 300 Fourth Street office building, and 730 Harrison Street, which was honored by the California Art Deco Society for its historic reinterpretation of art deco themes and its distinctive use of glazed terra-cotta exterior cladding.

JS: How did the Kiiroihana restaurant job in San Francisco's North Beach come about?

LH: We do a lot of restaurant jobs. The owners had seen a Japanese restaurant I had done across the street and contacted me about doing work for them. My main contact was Japanese and not fluent in English, so everything went through a translator. He told me he really liked my Japanese restaurants because they look so Western.

JS: Because they look so Western?

LH: Yes. My non-Japanese clients come to me and say they love my Japanese restaurants because they look so Japanese. It's a nice marriage. The editor of a restaurant magazine in L.A. called me about publishing the job, and said it was better than anything he had seen. He said, "I got your name and was shocked to find out you're not Japanese. Obviously, you've been to Japan, because the restaurant is a lot like what's going on now there." I had been there a number of years ago.

JS: What did you see in Japan that you put into this job?

LH: Almost everything they do is done beautifully in a graphic sense and has such a wonderful feeling for color, material, and texture. That's something I've always enjoyed as well. I have always been very heavily into graphics. Because of that, we end up doing an approach that includes graphics. For example, the graphics on the back wall of Kiiroihana are actually traditional Japanese emblems called *mon*.

JS: What's their derivation?

LH: They're used as ornament. Some of them have separate meanings. They're used a million different ways. At the restaurant, their layout was designed during working drawings, as well as the graphic layout of the neon. The largest of the emblems on the wall is actually my monogram. The client questioned the symbols when he saw them on the drawings. I explained to him that one of them was my symbol, and they said fine. It's very Japanese to sign your work. Another of the symbols on the wall, the double squares—one solid square and one with a circle in it—actually relates to the design of the double columns in the restaurant. The circle represents a five-inch sewer main uncovered during construction coming down the demising wall between the original two spaces. It paralleled the column. We couldn't afford to move it because that would have involved three floors of residential units above the restaurant. I was faced with a situation where I had a mess of problems to deal with and something that was very visible. I went through, I don't know, a half-dozen schemes, double columns and this and that, all based on the plumbing problem. I was frantic one night during design and asked one of the guys, "What am I going to do here?" He suggested, rather timidly, that I just repeat the existing square column. It all came together instantly. It was fabulous.

JS: It's very elegant.

LH: I like to think of the double column as a stylized samurai. They're very graphic, and they stand as a piece of sculpture within the place.

We have done a number of jobs for this client, some renovation work. This is the finest of the work done for them, a full-blown effort. I had control of the whole thing from the start, which I requested because we had done a larger restaurant for them in Cupertino during which we had many problems. The sushi chef kept changing the details on the sushi bar. Things like that. So, I requested one client contact this time. If they wanted to change something, they had to come to me to do it. They agreed, and this was the outcome. I think they sensed the work was of a certain quality, so they asked for a lot of elaboration, which was nice.

Right and bottom: Kiiroihana Restaurant,
San Francisco

Backen Arrigoni and Ross

Robert Arrigoni

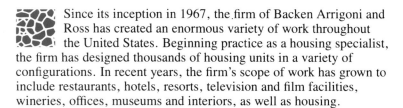

Top and bottom left: Glickman Residence, San Francisco.

Since its inception in 1967, the firm of Backen Arrigoni and Ross has created an enormous variety of work throughout the United States. Beginning practice as a housing specialist, the firm has designed thousands of housing units in a variety of configurations. In recent years, the firm's scope of work has grown to include restaurants, hotels, resorts, television and film facilities, wineries, offices, museums and interiors, as well as housing.

JS: What is the evolution of your design attitudes at BAR?

RA: We started out as modernists. Most of our early buildings were modernist but our educational background is pretty well steeped in the history of architecture. We have always been very much interested in every aspect of architecture. We studied Edwin Luytens and all those other people before they ever became fashionable. We've never been interested in developing a BAR style. If we get into one thing for too long we really get tired of it. We still think and work in an abstract language, but the buildings have a definite stylistic reality about them because there is such strong, programmatic client input to a lot of what we do, and, usually, strong context.

For example, we've done things like the Jordan Winery, north of San Francisco, which is modelled on a Bordeaux wine estate. At least, it has those clothes. In reality, it's a pretty sophisticated piece of architecture in terms of the way it works on the site and its spatial organization.

JS: How did the form of it come about?

Above: Glickman Residence, San Francisco.

Below: Glickman Residence, San Francisco.

RA: What was built is only the first phase. There was going to be a very high-quality inn and restaurant built in conjunction with the winery, forming a large courtyard built out over the view to the vineyards. The winery and the wine are so successful that the client didn't feel it necessary to construct the inn. The original design of the winery was more like the formal château at a Bordeaux estate. But the building became more of a hybrid and is now somewhat picturesque. We were able to convince the client that her desire for a Bordeaux-style winery wouldn't be reflected in a formal château. Bordeaux winery buildings are really very simple barnlike structures. We were criticized at the time for taking jobs like the Jordan Winery.

JS: By people in the profession?

RA: Yes, exactly. But, we'd say, "The guy wants a French château, OK? We're going to give him the best one we can do." We've done a lot of jobs like that. Skywalker

Above: detail, private residence, Oakland.

Facing page top: Macondray Terrace Condominiums, San Francisco. This photo illustrates the view corridor developed for units in the building at the rear of the photograph. Bottom: Raffinelli Residence, Piedmont.

Ranch, for example. George Lucas has developed a storyline for the ranch, which we follow. It's an imaginary script about how the ranch came into its present form. It goes something like: "The ranch belonged to an old family in Marin, who lived in the big house. George bought it and remodeled the house into his film studio and turned the winery into the technical building." And so on. When we work there we have to develop storyboards, just as you do in a movie. So, in a way Skywalker Ranch is designed as a collection of scenes. Many of the buildings have parts that look like they've been remodeled from something else. We also do projects like the Marin Tennis Club, which is a very simple box, very inexpensive, very modernist. Obviously, if you were Richard Meier you wouldn't have that flexibility. You would screw up your image. That's kind of sad to us. Every project for us is entirely different. In our view that makes the way we practice very difficult, because we have to shift from job to job and learn and work with a new vocabulary for each project. We recognize that we're limiting our chances of getting published by not being consistent stylistically. We have many excellent projects that have never been published. One of them is Macondray Lane, an apartment complex on Russian Hill.

It attempts to reconcile the many different styles on its block. At the time, we were sick of the bay window syndrome and tried to pick up on a building type that's common in San Francisco. We wanted to see what we could do with it.

JS: What was that type?

RA: I would call it something between Mediterranean and craftsman, but of stucco and not of shingles or another wood finish. The interesting thing about the building is that the client was in a lawsuit with the adjacent homeowners on a previous design because of blocked views. What we did was meet with the homeowners and develop a design that satisfied their concerns. Our surveyor got up into all their units and surveyed the view angles from which we devel-

oped an outside envelope. We had to get a variance to get all of the required open space into a center courtyard to open up the main view corridor. By doing this the opponents to the project dropped their suit and supported the project unanimously. It was a case of us acting as mediator/architects.

JS: So, you very nicely solved the problems of context and design review. What do you think of the expanding powers of the design review process for buildings in San Francisco?

RA: I would say that it is too late. In the 60s in San Francisco there was a great deal of growth. A lot of fine buildings were demolished to make way for some really bad buildings. I can't think of a worse group of new buildings as a whole than we have in San Francisco. Would you agree?

JS: I think there are quite a few disasters at the end of California Street and from the south side of Market Street on into the South-of-Market area.

RA: They're just horrible, absolutely horrible. Many fine buildings were removed in the name of growth. I think it's almost too late, but they've now developed legislation to try to solve the problem.

JS: What is the future for BAR?

RA: We have developed a very unique expertise in film, video, and sound-related facilities. Probably second to none, through our work with George Lucas and Disney. We're going after a lot more of that work. But my partners and myself are simple people. We don't like to travel, and we're not interested in making speeches, going to clubs, and talking to anybody about our work. We simply enjoy what we're doing and we have fun doing it.

Right: Jordan Winery, Alexander Valley.

David Baker Architects

David Baker

 University of California, Berkeley graduate David Baker began his practice in Berkeley designing coffeehouses and speculative office buildings for the area around Telegraph Avenue. Recently relocated in San Francisco's South-of-Market area, his work includes many low-cost housing projects throughout the Bay Area.

Right: Cody's Cafe, Berkeley.

JS: As an example of how you work, how did you relate the housing project you designed on Frederick Street to San Francisco?

DB: The units are based on low-cost, typical Victorian flats which make the San Francisco pattern. Victorian flats are not spectacular, just very livable. They're generic.

The project faces Golden Gate Park. There are three-story buildings on the street edge that are very different from Victorians in that they allow for entry into the site for cars and people. The site is permeable, as opposed to another pattern language of San Francisco, which has an enclosed garden in the middle with a wall of Victorians around it.

My practice has two distinct components, one of which is housing. It's really hard to do a good housing project. Look at the Western Addition and you can see that. I think it's impossible to do something that looks vernacular, as though it was built over time. It never looks that way. The other approach is that you make everything look exactly the same. That seemed to be what people did in the 60s and 70s, when there was a real crisis in terms of what people were doing.

JS: I think so, too.

DB: This is a more open period. We have the excesses of postmodernism, but it still opened the whole book again for architects. You can design something for other reasons than the flow diagram of the garbage to the dumpster. The housing I do tends to be very contextual, and that's for a number of reasons. The projects are for beginning-income people who are starting out on their own, so the housing is very soft-spoken and contextual and not striving at all. They're all low scale and I suppose postmodern. I know everybody hates that word, but the work I've done within existing San Francisco neighborhoods is contextual postmodernism. I think that doing something else would just be inappropriate. However, in the commercial work I've done it certainly hasn't been that way. I really feel more like a modernist. I mean, I would never use an Ionic column. Even in the golden age of columns, I could never bring myself to do it.

Left: Cody's Cafe, Berkeley.

JS: Is the Frederick Street project wood frame over a concrete parking garage?

DB: No. I have an unusual background in that I was a carpenter and actually built some houses I designed. That's why I've been able to work quite well in the affordable housing realm, because I have a pretty good idea of how to make things more economical in the basic concept. In this case, what I've done is to provide individual garages. They're not only more economical, but people really like them. Anyone can enter their own unit through the garage.

JS: That's great. I've never seen that in a large multiunit project.

DB: The first one I did like this was in Sacramento. What is amazing is that single women would buy these places. You'd talk to them afterwards and they'd say, "I can come home. I'm safe, my car doesn't get stolen. I don't get assaulted because I can get into my house."

This kind of solution does make the site grading difficult. Distributing cars all around the site and having multiple entries requires large, flat areas, whereas, with one large garage you only need one entry. One large garage also reduces the need for retaining walls.

JS: I've driven by the site and noticed that you're saving the magnificent old buildings on either end of the block. What are they?

DB: They're the old boys' and girls' gyms for Polytechnic High, which we demolished to make way for the project. They're great buildings. My impression is that they must have been designed by refugees from Pflueger's office in San Francisco in the early 30s who ended up in a government work program. Whoever did the design really understood detailing. The project was done during the Depression, so at that time there must have been a lot of good designers from his office floating around without a job. Perhaps some of them ended up on the Poly

Above top and bottom: Hodgkin Hall, Berkeley.

High project. Those buildings are slated to become the community center.

JS: I think providing good, low-cost public housing, such as you are doing at the Frederick Street project, is very difficult. Our training sometimes precludes developing the ability to create appropriate solutions. I spoke with Henrik Bull, who admires Hassan Fathy for his low-cost buildings in Egypt that seem to be developed from within the problem rather than from outside of it.

DB: As architects we are trained to think in an intellectual way that often has no real application when we get out of school. People have to separate reality from intellectual issues. That isn't to say that intellectual issues aren't important. Of course, many of them are. The problem is that in architecture the kind of thinking one learns often leads to inappropriate solutions. That's what happened when many architects in the early twentieth century tried to design workers' housing. The workers hated it. If you really want to provide housing for people, you should buy them mobile homes.

JS: Your designs for Cody's Café and Café Milano in Berkeley seem to have much more of a basis in "high style" than your housing work.

DB: I don't want to sound too much like Ace Architects, but I think style is a pretty unimportant thing to be concerned with. There is good work being done in every style. They come in and out of fashion. The projects, Cody's and Café Milano, are strongly contextualist. The way they are designed is as if they are a matrix, or overlay of ideas. They happened over quite a period of time, which produced their richness. I think that the basic thing, though, is that they are eclectic modernism.

JS: Cody's seems to be partly about the meeting of late Konstantin Melnikov and Adolph Loos. Kind of like the Cadillac ads in the 50s. I can see a Cadillac with tail fins on the floor right now. Some of your other modernist designs seem very fragmented.

DB: What I like is that when you take something apart and break it into pieces you can reassemble it differently. Whereas, if you make everything into one piece, it becomes seamless. I like the conflict between broken and divided things and elegantly resolving that conflict.

JS: Aren't you engaging in the academic intellectualizing you criticize?

DB: To me it's visceral. I went to school in the 70s when you weren't really supposed to explain why you did things, because you were supposed to do everything in a practical way. I did a project at Cal that had an arched entry. I was roasted during the entire critique because an arch supposedly wasn't natural in concrete. The school was full of that kind of thinking and wouldn't allow anything you couldn't intellectually explain. One way of thinking about architecture that greatly impressed me, and was quite different from what I heard in school, was what Michael Graves said about his design for the Clos Pegase winery. I feel very ambivalent about his work, but his logical and intellectual foundations for his work are very eloquent.

JS: I've heard him talk and read some of what he's written. What he says and writes is very rich, even if one disagrees with the solution.

DB: In contrast to some of the architects who explained their designs for the winery around the circulation pattern for the forklifts, Graves spoke about Pegasus flying down to strike the mountain so that a spring came forth. That was his explanation for the spring in his design. That's an exciting idea, and I really respect it. It's much more exciting to talk about Pegasus flying down to strike the mountain than building circulation. I still think, though, that the ultimate experience is visceral. When you become too intellectual about your designs, they can age in a really unpleasant way. It's important to have well-developed ideas in your work, not only in the way Graves does but in the different ways many of us do. Still, though, the ultimate point of architecture is passion, the subconscious feeling of rightness, wonder, and excitement.

Right: Park View Commons, San Francisco.

Right and below: Hodgkin Hall, Berkeley.

Left and bottom: Knipshild Residence by Batey and Mack, Sonoma Valley. The top photograph includes the eyebrow over the entry columns.

Andrew Batey

 With Mark Mack, his partner until 1985, Andrew Batey created a number of homes in the Bay Area and in other parts of America as well that have influenced a generation of architects looking for a modern architecture that respects tradition, climate, and modern construction. His own journey in architecture has taken him from England, where he was educated, to Mexico, and recently to the California College of Arts and Crafts where he acted as Dean of Architecture from 1987 to 1989.

JS: Your career in architecture has been quite an adventure so far. Could you summarize it?

AB: I'm from California's Central Valley. I studied architectural history in England at Oxford, graduating in 1968. From there I went to Cambridge to study architecture and had the most orthodox modernist education you could have. Cambridge in the 60s was the last bastion of straight modernism. Leslie Martin ran the school, and I luckily avoided the chaos of the East Coast, the opening of Pandora's box. I graduated from Cambridge in 1971.

JS: What do you mean by that?

AB: I mean that history became the main vehicle for architectural education and eclecticism became a possibility. That was not the case with my education. It was rigid and straight modernist, and in that sense a classical education.

JS: I agree with you that a certain kind of rigor in the modernist education we received in architecture before the mid-70s has gone out of architectural education today.

AB: Cambridge was the last place left. Norman Foster, Richard Rogers, and James Stirling were all teaching there. When I arrived, Peter Eisenman had just left as a student. I was the next American to follow that whirlwind, which is a very hard act to follow. When I left Cambridge I worked for Foster, who was the most sympathetic of the teachers.

JS: How so?

AB: To me he was the gentlest and most open to thoughts about the environment. All the things I thought were important issues as a student were conveyed by Foster as a teacher, although his work didn't necessarily convey the same issues. I worked for him for a year and then returned to California and did a house in Berkeley for Henry Bowles. But the mentor thing was still very important to me. I decided I was awash in California. So, I went to Mexico and knocked on Luís Barragan's door. For the next two and a half years I went back and forth working for Luís. It completely overshadowed the Foster experience.

JS: I didn't know you worked for Barragan. It's the missing link for me in an understanding of your work.

AB: Yes, it is the missing link. When I came to California from England something was missing in the architecture here and it wasn't something in California. I loved Joseph Esherick's work, but there seemed to be something missing that was appropriate to California. In those days Charles Moore was the biggest influence in the Bay Area. The only architect I could think of who did something essentially Californian was Irving Gill, although that was in southern California.

JS: What is it that is essentially Californian in Gill's architecture?

AB: It's a recognition of the climate and the tradition. I felt an affinity with Gill. I also felt that my training in orthodox modernism had given me a foundation in this sort of Loosian rigor.

I had a tough time with the so-called Bay Area style being done at that time. To me, much of it seemed to be a caricature of the real Bay Area style. As it was often practiced in the 60s and 70s, the Bay Area style allowed a lot of ridiculous things. There was a proliferation of trellising and a wooliness of the plan and parti. Eclecticism works in the hands of someone who really understands it, like Maybeck, but most of the architects trying to do something that was somehow or other authentic to the area for that time used the more obvious design elements, such as trellising, in a decorative way that in no way reflected any real understanding of what the Bay Area style could be. The architects I gravitated to here, such as Don Olsen and Dan Solomon, it seemed to me, had the germ of a more severe and appropriate architecture. So, Barragan was very appealing to me.

JS: What was it like to work for him?

AB: The education I had working for him is unsurpassable. Those of us who worked for him lived and worked in the same space. The whole ritual of life was the architecture. It was something you had to learn.

When I returned and began working in the Napa Valley, I did some very Barragan-inspired buildings, which were clumsy, inappropriate, and out-of-sync.

JS: When you moved beyond the overt imitations of Barragan, what stayed with you?

AB: I learned a lot about color and light from him that stayed with me, and I think over the years I have increasingly become a minimalist. When Mark Mack and I practiced together we tried to set up a polemic that included those influences and be true to it, which was very hard to do in the heady days of postmodernism.

Above: Knipshild House by Batey and Mack, Sonoma Valley.

Since we've split up, I'm tending towards minimalism and a more abstemious, severe approach. Some architects have taken a somewhat similar approach, but the result is often deliberate crudity and ugliness. In fact, the work is often uncomfortable and slightly uneasy-making. That is in contrast to what I think is the best of Bay Area architecture, which is its combining of comfort and tradition with modernism, without being aggressive about it.

JS: I think there is an unwritten history of Bay Area architecture that would concentrate on the history, development, and assimilation of modernism. It's never been well explained. It's quite strong.

AB: Definitely. Richard Neutra built two homes in San Francisco that both look like they belong here. I think Esherick was the turning point, in that he broke down the overt modesty of William Wurster and started playing with the elements.

JS: Your own education is somewhat similar. You worked for a very modern architect, in his use of technology, and for an architect who designed buildings that were both modern and uniquely appropriate to their setting.

AB: I feel very lucky to have studied with two masters. Usually in architecture school and afterwards you don't have that chance. My success in architecture is attributable to having worked for them and having them as father figures. Who you have worked for is part of your own architecture, and the best architecture is autobiographical. It's not about something abstract. It's certainly not about history one has no connection to, such as a Roman palace or a Palladian villa. I think the reckless quotation of architecture gives you nothing. Livermore is not the place for Tuscan houses. Architecture is about what you've experienced and that is where I've found architectural education really lacking.

JS: As an educator, how are you trying to fill that void?

AB: I'm trying to develop a European program at school. I have always attempted to see history as totally integral to design. But it has to be tenable, whether it's the history of California, or Gill, or traveling, or the house next door. My thesis at school was on Palladio, and I lived in the Villa Malcontenta for a month. Part of the education of architects up to the twentieth century was the grand tour, when you went, drew, and learned from built history. I'm trying to make it possible for students to do that.

JS: What about the studio courses?

AB: As a dean I developed a very different approach and point of view than when I was a studio critic. I have come to believe that the studio, the creative element, is less and less important in architecture school than the underpinnings, than the decent, ordered structures of building systems and history.

I taught a studio with Michael Graves at Princeton for a semester. It was very revealing because it was a copy book exercise, which most studios end up being. That's not very helpful in

the accumulation of architectural knowledge. You have to work the design things out yourself, and they may or may not come. There is one real designer in a thousand. The responsibility of architectural education today is similar to that of the Beaux Arts system. You learn what you have to learn, you get a mentor, and you learn from him. My Cambridge architectural education only worked because it was combined with my degree in architectural history from Oxford. I was, at least, prepped to be able to get the hard facts down knowing that I had some perspective on what the world of architecture is all about.

JS: Andrew, I want to ask you about a specific project, the Knipshild House.

AB: The Knipshild House is the reason I quit architecture for a period in 1985. It was the final blow.

JS: What happened?

AB: One day I arrived at the site during construction. There was an eyebrow that wasn't supposed to be there over an opening. I said, "Take it off." They said, "How are we going to protect the tops of these columns from the rain?" They were detailed properly on the working drawings. A foot-and-a-half eyebrow is not going to protect the columns from the rain.

JS: Did they take it off?

AB: No. The tiniest little things can change the character. I have problems with architects when little issues become so important and they throw in the towel and quit the profession. But, for me, this was the straw that broke the camel's back. There are a number of houses that we've done with very fortlike blank façades, almost nonfaçades that are penetrated with something happening on the other side. This was one of them and that eyebrow was all wrong.

JS: That particular aspect of the house?

AB: Yes, that tiny thing more than anything. I turned forty almost to the day. I got a divorce, Mark and I split up, I sold my architectural library to Bill Stout and walked out. I went to Europe saying, "This is the last of this thing. I'm going to design underwear."

JS: What did you do in Europe?

AB: I did what was very appropriate for the time. I worked on a book I am still writing entitled *Places of Refuge*. It's about houses and other places people escape to, places of retreat. Historically, artists, writers, kings, and princes have had refuges. The book is anecdotal and includes such varied places as castles and Napoleon's tent.

JS: And from there you came back to San Francisco.

AB: Yes. I was dean of architecture at the California College of Art and Crafts for a year and a half. I resigned as dean because it took a tremendous amount of time I did not have, but I have stayed on at the school as a kind of philosophical guru.

New Architecture

Bigelow/Edwards Architects

Christopher Bigelow

Christopher Bigelow received a Master of Architecture degree from the University of California at Berkeley in 1980. He has maintained an active involvement in the arts, designing stage sets for dance, as a member of Business Volunteers for the arts, and is the chairman of the board of directors of Intersection for the Arts in San Francisco. Prior to becoming an interior designer and architect he was a dancer for many years in New York City.

JS: What was it like for you to partially remodel a building designed by noted Bay Area architect William Wurster?

CB: I felt very fortunate to be able to work within a framework established by someone like Wurster. I was quite conscious of the difference between my own design inclinations and his. The project of remodeling the kitchen and bath seemed like a good opportunity to create a dialogue between the little spaces in what is a very compact house. In general there is a nice contrast between the details and materials of the new spaces we remodeled and the spaces we didn't do much to except paint. We used paint to call out forms, such as the finwall around which the stair wraps. I tried to take a light touch in approaching Wurster but felt ready to introduce new materials and design ideas in the spaces I was working in.

JS: I think you've created some strong contrasts, especially in the way the front corner of the kitchen is detailed. The way the column is inserted into the composition acts as an introduction to a vocabulary that you don't normally find in a Wurster building.

CB: The new work is actually a combination of new details, details that are an extension of what I found in Wurster, like the molding. I responded very carefully to the details I found in the house. They were pretty minimal, but I was careful to duplicate the size of moldings around doors and the setbacks between door casings and frames. I let them create the module of reveals that are in the opening between the sitting area and the kitchen. I was very intrigued about how the new details would accommodate each other, and that accommodation resulted in the system of reveals and setbacks.

JS: The detailing of the corner is provocative. I can see it blown up in size to the corner of an office building. The scale can be multiplied easily.

CB: Change the scale and you get urban.

JS: What was the design problem at the Cameraworks Gallery?

CB: They had an existing structure in the west gallery that accommodates an archival library

and a preparation area into which they wanted to add display space for art books. The idea was to insert a new element as a third space bridging between two spaces and let it have a presence that was quite different from the surrounding walls. The vocabulary of the exposed studs is drawn from the exposed ceiling framing in the space. The new work will not only relate to the existing context but will also serve as a defined but open space that will invite entry.

JS: Why does the highest point of the pediment intersect the header?

CB: I thought that point was very critical. I could have held it below, or attached it to another element. What I wanted to do was strengthen the experience of the new area as a third space bridging two existing spaces. The proximity of the header to the gable allowed me to do this.

JS: Your work has a remarkable amount of thoughtful detail to it. For example, the way the glass-front cabinets are put together.

CB: Those hardware items were a combination of a couple of things I took from disparate bins in different hardware stores. I find myself frequently doing that.

JS: You've begun your career in architecture fairly late. How has your former career as a dancer affected your architecture?

CB: My training as a dancer and my attention to how body parts fit together has influenced my interest in the way materials and forms in architecture relate to each other. I also have a choreographic sensibility about planning spatial relationships. It's hard for me to express, but I think it's evident, for example, in the corner we were talking about in the kitchen in terms of how its elements fit together and move in space.

JS: Can you put into words what the heart of the design problem is for you?

CB: At the core of each act of design I find myself trying to explore the relationships within a set of opposing forces. That's important to me. If there is no inherent tension in a project, I'll invariably introduce a contradictory element to the mix to create a conscious interaction with the built environment where there was none before. The effort isn't necessarily to balance the forces but to choreograph their interaction.

Above: Bigelow Residence, San Francisco.

Right and below: Bigelow Residence, San Francisco.

Bull Volkmann Stockwell

Henrik Bull

Bull Volkmann Stockwell was recently named the 1989 California Council American Institute of Architects firm of the year. Composed of thirty persons and located in San Francisco's North Beach, the firm is well known for its designs for ski area projects as well as hotel design and a wide variety of other work. Henrik Bull, Sherwood Stockwell, and Robert Allen own and manage the firm and are active in the design of all projects.

JS: I read in *Bay Area Houses* a description of your inspirations to come to the Bay Area. According to the text, it applies also to Charles Moore. It says, "The picturesque image of the redwoodsy boxes with stovepipe chimneys tied to the roofs and decks like trays over the void inspired in them a deep longing to come West." Today we might interpret that as a deep desire to become a deconstructivist.

HB: I think it's a case of somebody else's words, because I have never been fond of stovepipes attached with wires. In fact, I don't think we've ever done anything like that. Before coming out here I wrote to four architects. They were Joseph Esherick, Mario Corbett, Worley Wong, and William Wurster. I got a job with Corbett, and after one summer's work he offered me a partnership. So, when I got out of the Air Force I came out here to be his partner. I knew that Mario had been married six times, but not that he had had at least as many partners over the years. Our partnership lasted six weeks, until the work ran out. But, Mario's work influenced me greatly, as it did Charles Moore, who also worked for him.

JS: How did it influence you?

HB: Corbett had absolutely no architectural hangups. He had never been to architectural school and so in that sense was unspoiled. The solutions to the individual buildings were all unique, a wild variety. It was very exciting. He could never put into words what he meant by this or that. Some of them were quite formal, while others were quite wild. All strong designs.

JS: Did Corbett influence you in the direction of regionalism?

HB: Very definitely. The most lasting influence, though, was Esherick's early houses—the ground-hugging buildings scattered through the Central Valley and Marin County. They respected the site so beautifully and looked like they had always been there, which is an attitude we respect as an office. We don't care if it isn't a fresh, brand new solution. If it looks like it belongs, as if it grew there, we're

Above: Visitor Center, Point Reyes.

happy, because that's what we're striving for. We're probably one of the few offices that would not cringe at being called romantics.

JS: What do you mean by "romantic"?

HB: For one thing, I mean architecture that evokes fond memories of a historic nature.

JS: What about your own work is romantic?

HB: I think almost all of the projects we've done that you can see on the conference room walls in the office are romantic. For example, we have drawings on the wall for Squaw Valley that are meant to suggest an alpine village, one that uses the common sense of hundreds of years of dealing with the elements. We're proposing removing the parking lot at Squaw and putting ten thousand people into that area. The idea of getting away from the cars completely is a romantic idea. Zermatt is perhaps the most romantic ski resort, just as Venice is the most romantic tourist town. There are no cars, and that makes for a very different kind of feeling. Romantic is romantic is romantic. Warren Callister's work has always been very romantic.

JS: In your article in the March/April 1988 issue of *Architecture California* you say that ". . . when the Beaux Arts tradition was vanquished by the modernist crusade, architecture related to natural surroundings found refuge in the Bay Area." Further along, you say, "At that time Bay Area architecture was characterized by casual elegance, the use of natural materials, and the frank expression of structure, ideas more Japanese than classical European."

HB: Now, of course, the Japanese have taken over the Corbusian tradition. Their original tradition has disappeared in the chaos.

JS: What is the value of being aligned with the attitude known as regionalism?

HB: I can't understand an architecture that isn't regional.

JS: I've talked with some architects who can't understand one that is.

HB: Right, and they put up the same dumb box in Greenwich and Timbuctou. Richard Meier is the master of the white box. It doesn't change, wherever it is.

JS: Perhaps it's unreasonable to expect architecture to be strongly regional today, because there are such strong ties between different parts of the country and the world. Perhaps with television, jet travel, and the great proliferation of books, videos, and other information, regionalism has lost much of its meaning.

HB: I don't buy that at all. Something that is built in a harsh climate should show that, just as a building constructed in a desert climate should reflect that climate. I think much of the chaos in the world and the really bad architecture has come from the whole Corbusian movement, and the work of Gropius, that made modern architecture a religion. The beauty of vernacular architecture—another expression I'm not ashamed of—is that there is a unity to a village that has a tradition of building. That tradition came from dealing with the elements, which we still have to do. There is also a unity and continuity from using the materials around us, instead of shipping steel all over the world. Do you know the work of Hassan Fathy?

JS: Yes, I do. He's an Egyptian architect who builds fine buildings very cheaply, often for the poor.

HB: I really respect him because he recognizes that housing for poor people uses cheap materials, the ones you find outside your door. The typical architectural school approach is to ship in precast concrete, which is tough when there are no roads. That doesn't make any sense.

JS: Frank Lloyd Wright called Bay Area architecture something like a bunch of dumb sheds. That isn't the exact quote, but he had the idea that if something was vernacular in a picturesque sense or reduced to a stereotypical form it wasn't fine architecture.

HB: I remember the quote. In fact I spent a day with Frank Lloyd Wright for fifty bucks, around 1958 or 1959, just before he died. It was fantastic. I agree with him to a large extent. I think a lot of the Wurster houses, particularly the ones in the late 40s and 50s were really very expensive shacks. That wasn't what brought me out here.

I don't mind shacks like the Point Reyes barn, because barns are barns. I think I'm a rationalist in the old-fashioned sense, not the modern sense, meaning that I think the building ought to solve the problem the best way possible. When I interviewed for the Point Reyes job I saw there were going to be a lot of spaces that needed to be dark—the exhibit spaces, the automated slide-show, and so on—while other spaces needed light. Those two things fit very well with the program. I told them, "If you hire us, chances are the building will be a barn form. I think I can sell that to all the people who won't want anything built." I would have opposed it if it didn't look like it had always been there.

Below: Visitor Center, Point Reyes.

Callister, Gately, Heckmann & Bischoff

Charles Warren Callister

 Born in Rochester, New York, and reared in Texas, Charles Warren Callister practices architecture and community design with his firm near the Tiburon waterfront on San Francisco Bay. Callister began his Bay Area office in 1946. The firm does commercial, development, and residential projects from coast to coast.

JS: My impression of your work is that it relies a great deal on the intuitive.

WC: I'm not so sure in the usual sense. I think the intuitive aspect develops out of selected remembrances as well as from knowledge and experience. It depends; it may not need explanation. I subscribe to *Art in America* and find the photographs and reproductions very provocative, but I think the explanatory discussions by the critics are funny. They're just hilarious when they speculate about what the artist was trying to do or was sensing. I can imagine the artist saying, "Oh, my god, I didn't think of that, I didn't know I was supposed to have thought that."

JS: What do you think of an architectural approach that insists on using stripped-down archetypal forms and allows for little that is idiosyncratic? Something like rationalism?

WC: Our approach is quite different, although our work has an element of the rational. I think there is a current emphasis in the universities that creates architects interested in puzzling things out but not necessarily being creative. The resulting design tends to be analytical in nature. You do achieve a resultant solution by such a method, but I think you have to add a great deal more substance.

JS: What do you mean when you say a great deal of substance is left out?

WC: I think it has to do with standing back from what you're doing and seeing the work relative to the relationships you've had in the process of producing the design, which I think are most important. Those relationships can range from the most profound to those that are absolutely superficial.

For example, I think substance can be found in your relationship to where you are working geographically. I don't like the word "regional" more than any other architectural jargon, but I suggest that we should try to stay within the cultural mood and appropriateness relative to the architectural setting we are relating to. If we don't, a great deal is lost.

When I studied new housing in Europe, I visited a number of countries to try to discover the differences in multifamily residential architecture. Most of what I found were similarities, which was discouraging. It was later suggested that I visit China to see their new housing, but, I said, "I don't know that I need to."

JS: You wouldn't find many differences.

WC: They mostly seem to look the same. I'm searching to find distinctions that critics would probably judge as not being as important within the international sense of architectural fashion. One of my colleagues, Jim Bischoff, is very conscious of what we might gain by designing relative to journalistic persuasions, and I can see that may be of some importance. There are some commercial projects that can be looked at in the terms of periodic but very temporary trends in design, such as the ever-changing trends in the design of restaurant projects.

JS: Are you equating commercial with being more international in scope?

WC: No, I'm equating it with being more stylized. We've done restaurants often in the manner requested by our clients that would seem to be necessarily in vogue. A friend of mine said that every four years we have a new decade of architectural style. When I talk to students, I ask them if they are choosing motifs from the architectural magazines. I point out to them that if they are, they should look upon their work as the result of current trends in journalism. The problem with spending too much time and interest in temporary trends of design is that the student or the architect does not project a larger, more creative comprehensive vision.

JS: When you talk about substance, you mention the regional setting. What gives this such a special quality or mood?

WC: The Japanese ocean current off our coast creates a climate here that induces a certain cultural mood from Alaska to Point Conception, California. In part because of the natural inheritance this Pacific coast has evolved with many similar qualities of the Pacific orient. The abundance of timber has created an architecture of wood somewhat similar in its use as in Japan. San Francisco Bay Area architecture is certainly within the realm of Asian-Pacific influences both naturally and culturally.

JS: In your own work, how do you create work that goes beyond stylistic concerns?

WC: It's not style nor the techniques of building but the "process" of doing architecture with others that develops and creates work that goes beyond such concerns. The nature of the client in this process partnership is most important. Today some of our clients, even young clients, are very conservative. For now, we are responding to their conservative views because it is part of the ongoing adventure of creating architecture.

Above: private residence, Stinson Beach.

Top and bottom left: private residence, Stinson Beach.

Financial advantages have suddenly come to many people who seem to wish that their envisioned manner of living had some history, so they concern themselves with traditional forms. Architects need to point out that there is a more imaginative, beautiful, and adventuresome heritage of another kind that architecture can express. We need to move away from the superficially pretentious toward an architecture that reflects important social, cultural, and aesthetic achievements.

JS: An outcome of the rapid Bay Area population growth was the Tiburon building moratorium in 1986, which stopped new construction for two years while various studies were undertaken. From your vantage point of practicing architecture in Tiburon and Marin County for over forty years, and as a member of the local planning commission, what did you see transpire in those two years?

WC: There were many interesting outcomes. Principally that a community can't stop growth of traffic by a building moratorium nor can they stop population growth. One of the ironic aspects was the attempt of the Environmental Impact Report with its effort to accommodate and justify motor vehicles. The destruction of our environment by the automobile is not recognized by the public nor did the environmentalists condemn its extensive use nor analyze its disastrous impact in their EIR.

JS: EIRs are heavily into methodology and technique.

WC: I think it is important that such reports are involved in the spirit and meaning of "resolu-

tion" of planning matters. The technical is one aspect, but you can't find real planning solutions by way of technical environmental analysis. California planning law requires that we have a minimum of seven planning elements for the evaluation and formation of our General Plan of Development, but they leave out design.

JS: They leave out design?

WC: Yes, so I have asked that one of the aspects of environmental impact mitigation be "resolution" by way of design. And I have also asked that an architectural and engineering design element be included in our town's General Plan as a basis for implementation, and to restore the creative into the process of designing and developing our community.

Right facing page: private residence, Stinson Beach.

Right: private residence, Stinson Beach.

Susie Coliver

Arch, one of San Francisco's leading suppliers of materials and equipment to architects, is owned by Susie Coliver. She opened Arch in 1978 as a way to cover expenses during the inevitable slow periods of architectural practice. It has grown enormously since then. In addition to operating the store she has, since 1980, been associated with Robert Herman Associates, an architectural firm primarily involved with subsidized housing, libraries, and theaters. Susie Coliver is a native of San Francisco and a graduate of the University of California, Berkeley, where she has recently taught.

JS: Are the columns in Arch really old ships' masts?

SC: Yes. This is one of the oldest buildings in town, dating from 1853, when there were no lumber mills in the area. People would bring their ships around the Cape. When they arrived they dismantled them to use as building materials.

JS: How did the building survive the earthquake?

SC: It was the whiskey warehouse for the city. The firemen knew that and rushed over to sandbag the block during the fire, after the building had survived the earthquake. This is the oldest block in the city. There are a couple of little cottages on Telegraph Hill that are about as old.

JS: Didn't you find some very old Chinese figures on the walls?

Left and right: Arch, San Francisco.

SC: Yes. The previous life of this store was as a wallpaper wholesaler. When we got here, the walls were encrusted with nine or ten layers of the most awful floral prints, stripes, and unbelievable, dreadful wallpapers. The first thing we did was strip the walls. In doing so some of the plaster came off. Underneath it, we found Chinese figures. It was exciting, like archeology. The floor, similarly, was covered in dreadful linoleum, which we took down to the original underlay.

JS: The space you had to work with here is long and narrow. You played up the elongated dimension rather than try to conceal it.

SC: Making the space longer was something I was interested in. Shortly before starting on the space I had gone to a beauty salon to have them tell me how to do my face. The woman said we must color this this way and put some white and color there, to make my nose less long. She said I have a very long face, and if we highlight this and that it'll go a little more round. While she was talking I was thinking, Jesus Christ, if you've got a long face and you're blessed or cursed with a long nose, why not

acknowledge the fact and live with it. It's who you are.

JS: The store's design happened soon after this incident?

SC: Yeah. I thought, Well, if I'm not willing to do it to my nose, why should I do it to the store? It's such a funny notion to me to think that you should compensate for these givens instead of enhance them.

JS: I remember reading in your written description of the space something about your wanting the store to resemble a tightly crowded street. Why?

SC: I think all of us who graduated from architecture school in the last thirty years have had somebody mention the Italian hilltowns and what delights they hold. God knows we've heard it ad infinitum in every interview, in every article to the point of sickness. But nonetheless there is a fascination with things you can't see, things hidden around corners, and the enticing quality of sensing there is yet more to come. Because the store is so long and skinny, it set up as a street very nicely. I also wanted a lot of nooks and crannies people find by having to turn a corner or squeeze through an opening.

JS: How about other inspirations?

SC: I'd been to the David Hockney show at the museum where he recreated stage sets. There were a few you could actually walk into. That was tremendously emotional for me. I left saying, That's the drama I want people to experience when they walk into the store. What we sell is workaday stuff, which could have a negative association, and our supplies could be seen as tools of drudgery.

JS: Ninety-nine percent of drafting supply stores are like that.

SC: I wanted to take the drudge out of the workaday tools, so a recurring notion from the outset was to make a space that felt leisurely, that had leisure time associations. The tropics and the colors and a little mystery.

JS: So that's where the colors come from. I feel like I'm in a Stuart Davis painting when I'm in the store.

SC: I wanted it to be hot colors, not designer gray, black, and white, and a little touch of red, a tasteful touch. I wanted it to have associations relating to the places people go when they're not working. When I saw the Hockney stage sets they were very dramatic for me. I thought, We'll mix a little drama in with the leisure time activity and get a space people will actually enjoy coming to. I wanted a space associated with anything but deadlines and schedules, although what we do here is help people meet deadlines.

JS: You've certainly achieved that goal. In your article about the store, you mention historical reference and urban contextualism. . . .

SC: I do? I hope not. Those are dreadful words.

JS: Not in so many words, but those ideas are part of the thought in your article.

SC: Well, I'd like to go to that for a moment, because I'm not fond of historical contextualism.

What I think I'm interested in here is exploring those things about past built spaces that hold meaning for us today. If this space has any sense of history about it, I hope it's the elements themselves that make them appropriate in their time and delightful in our own. There's nothing here that has been borrowed from the past and lifted and placed in an applied manner. If it's a sense of history, it's because we're in an old building. I've left the oldness exposed, not brought it in from the outside. That's really important to me.

JS: I've never seen another store dealing in what you have here.

SC: I don't think there is one. I've looked around the country when I've traveled to see who else is doing a similar thing and haven't found anyone else. I get a certain satisfaction from thinking the store is what I set out for it to be. I think the greatest satisfaction for me as I get older is actually meeting my own mark.

Above: Arch, San Francisco.

Right and facing page: Arch, San Francisco.

ELS

Donn Logan and Carol Shen

 Donn Logan, Barry Elbasani, and Carol Shen, partners in ELS, direct the large Berkeley firm. ELS was established in 1967 when its partners won first prize in a national American Institute of Architects competition to design a civic center serving Binghamton, New York. Besides the Recreational Sports Facility pictured here, recent projects include the Portland Center for the Performing Arts in Portland, Oregon, and the Grand Avenue Retail Center in Milwaukee, Wisconsin. ELS also provides extensive planning and urban design services on such projects as the Glendale Downtown Urban Design Study and the Oakland Retail Center Study, which establishes development parameters for ten blocks of downtown Oakland.

JS: You went through a number of schemes for the recreation facility, didn't you?

ELS: We had many schemes, even including one that covered the swimming pool with a big sliding glass roof. Of course, as soon as they started looking at the dollars, the swimming pool roof was dropped. Most of the schemes had colonnades along the street. Some of them were more elaborate than the version built.

JS: Does the setback in the plan have anything to do with the relationship of the building to the church across the street?

ELS: That was a happy coincidence. Basically, we had a boundary set by the left field fence of the baseball field. The problem immediately became a game of fitting the building in between the street and the left field fence of the baseball field. Secondarily, we had an existing wall, the old wall from the original track stadium development, that many people wanted saved. Additionally, we had the constraint of circulating in and out of Harmon Gym. We set back the field house in order to create the exterior plaza that looks over the street to the church and the south sun. We put the parking underneath. I think the scheme is a very straightforward, functional, and modernist concept that provides the most efficient diagram to deal with the planning issues we could identify.

JS: Are you carrying the flag for an architecture based in function? The reason I ask is that I know you graduated from Arizona State University, as I did. When I graduated I knew there was more to building design than function, which was emphasized there, but it seemed no one there taught it. How has that affected you?

ELS: That school was free of theory. It tried to give you a valueless technique. It does take something more, obviously. You can join a movement or struggle with it personally, or whatever. We consider ourselves to be in the main stream of modernism. That does not mean that we are doctrinaire or immune from temporal stylistic influences. The background of the principals includes a heavy dose of CIAM, Team 10, and Japanese metabolism. Our teachers were people like Jose Luis Sert, Fumihiko Maki, Jerzy Soltan, and Willo Von Moltke. Our early work had strong-boned, somewhat diagrammatic concepts that could be seen as direct consequences of these influences. Later, the work became more textured, layered, and enriched. Some of this elaboration might be seen as attributable to the influences of postmodernism or rationalist neoclassicism. In a group practice it's hard to keep out all such impurities. However, I prefer to think that we are producing an architecture for the late twentieth century which might be called "expressive modernism."

JS: What are its characteristics?

ELS: First of all, it deals with the basics. That is, an architect should use a straightforward problem-solving approach. If you solve the problem and are sensitive to environment and context, it is still possible to make buildings that have a timeless quality and are up-to-date in style. Second, technology is OK. Structural expression is all right in some cases but not necessarily in every case. Mechanical expression is also all right, but not necessarily the thing to do in most buildings. Third, it is possible for buildings to be more decorated or more enriched while keeping their roots in the functional tradition of the modern movement. Many of our projects exhibit an interest in the surface graphics of walls, for instance.

JS: I want to ask you about something I don't understand. There don't seem to be any transitions from indoors to outdoors. It seems to happen quickly. I wonder about it because the building is in Berkeley and doesn't seem to acknowledge that fact, in this day and age of revived regionalism. Maybe that's not important to you. I thought one way you might do that is with a stronger indoor/outdoor transition, in the spirit of Bay Area regionalist work. The space between the building and the pool seems like a natural place for it.

ELS: You mean like a covered, outdoor space?

JS: Maybe, or a trellis. I don't know what it would be, perhaps overhangs. . . .

ELS: Not being a product of the Bay region tradition, I never thought about it that way. We don't normally do trellises in this office. The transition we accomplished is the little miniplaza, which is the forecourt to the entrance, where the doors are indented about six feet, so that there is a soffit overhead. Other than that we didn't feel the need to add anything to it. Of course, security raised its head both during design, and currently during management. It's the hardest building on campus to get into. We thought that people would wander in and out of the doors by the plaza, but they are locked tight, so the plaza doesn't get the activity it should.

JS: I've heard stressed many times in these interviews the value of anchoring a building in its specific place. These days there is a great emphasis on it. It's almost as though the profession has assumed a great burden of guilt for the so-called sins of the modernists, whose work to some was not "place-specific" enough.

ELS: I think we are interested in making things that are—and I hate to use the words you've been hearing, but—place-specific, and this building is place-specific. However, we are more interested in making buildings that can be generalized or viewed as perhaps existing someplace else, or as having lessons for someplace else. For instance, we're doing a building now in Phoenix that isn't going to be territorial, or Spanish colonial, or whatever. It's going to be a modernist building responding to the sun, heat, and the materials used in that area, as well as the way contractors build there.

JS: On the Berkeley recreation center you had a very difficult problem to handle all the required volume on such a thin site.

ELS: Yes. The setback part of the building is in response to that issue; we didn't want it all crowding the street. On the part of the building that comes forward to the sidewalk we dealt with the problem with an arcade. Our notion was that the arcade was part of the sidewalk, and an alternate route for walking down the street. Our idea was that people could look into the gym as they went down the walk. But that notion was sabotaged by the client's desire to block up the windows. We had windows looking into all of those rooms on the ground floor, which they didn't want. The management must think people inside the gym don't want to be seen. It's crazy. The people in Gold's Gym next to our office don't mind sitting in the window pedal-

ing an exerciser. That was the idea, that you could wander through the arcade and look into the gym.

JS: Now that you mention it, the way I saw any activity in the building was to poke my head in the doors of the gyms as I walked through it.

ELS: Exactly, but you have to get in through security first. The other thing about the massing is that the high part of the building is the same height as Harmon Gym, and the low part of the building is the same height as the low part of Harmon Gym, so that there is a formal tie-in at the cornice lines.

JS: On the elevations you also very nicely expressed the seismic bracing.

ELS: Yes. These façade patterns interest a lot of people. Some student journalists who wrote papers on it tried to describe it as postmodern and full of affectation. I just thought of it as a big volume with certain things going on. We've got steel bracing, we've got ventilation louvers, we've got a few other reveals, and we have to make a composition of what we've got to work with. That's all there is; it's a huge surface. We're not trying to decorate it so much as to make a composition out of all the pieces we had in the program. So, the height at which the mats are hung as well as the joints between them, and louver and duct locations and other functional necessities become the key elements to manipulate.

JS: How did you pick the colors?

ELS: It was a lengthy, purposeful process. The warm colors—the terra-cottas and the beiges—pick up the campus vernacular. Red tile roofs and such. The grayish, greenish, and bluish colors on the high parts of the building pick up some colors that you see on campus, such as copper roofs. The bluish colors on the high mass also help to diminish it a bit. It doesn't quite loom over the street the way it would if it were some hot color.

Facing page: Recreational Sports Facility, University of California, Berkeley.

Right: axonometric view, Recreational Sports Facility, University of California, Berkeley.

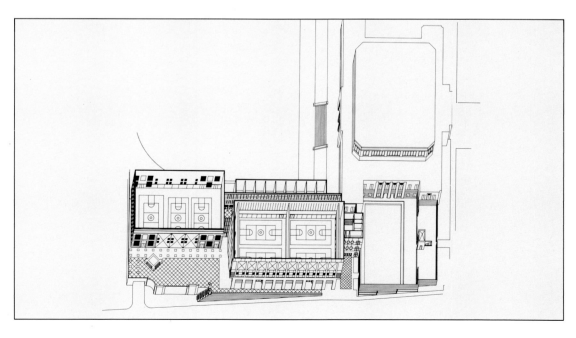

Fernau and Hartman Architects

Richard Fernau and Laura Hartman

Richard Fernau and Laura Hartman practice architecture from their office in Berkeley. Their work has been exhibited and published widely. Most recently, they were one of five firms included in the "Radical Regionalism" show at the San Francisco Arts Commission Gallery. In 1984 their Maoli House was included in the "Precocious Houses" exhibit at the Oakland Museum. Among their recent projects is the new student union for the University of California at Santa Cruz.

JS: What values do you think your buildings communicate?

F&H: "Modest audacity" is what we've often tried to convey, the oxymoronic quality, restraint and daring. That's what I would want you or anyone else viewing our work to be struggling with. We'd like people to perceive a restraint, a certain modesty, a sense that on one side architecture has certain limits, while having the ability to elevate the spirit on another. And that we're interested in the future far more than the past.

JS: Two of your houses, the Maoli House in San Rafael and the Bailey House in Kentfield, have a somewhat traditional domestic imagery, while the Berggruen House in Rutherford does not.

F&H: We want our work to be such that if you extracted those houses, just pulled them out of the ground and placed them somewhere, someone explaining them would have to describe the place they're from without relying on the visual imagery in order to place them. One of the values that we feel passionate about is of being someplace, being situated in that circumstance, and not trying to be anywhere else.

JS: You do communicate the sense of specific place in your work with imagery as well as more abstract means.

F&H: Because we play with some of the pieces, materials, and forms of the place, and allow them into the equation, it's almost like having an architectural death wish. I mean, we realize full well that if we use that stuff, we're potentially excommunicated from the College of the Avant Garde or the College of the Cutting Edge. But the edge that we want in the work is for it to be good enough that you don't want to throw it out, even though it touches the vernacular. I mean, the "colleges" see the value of the work, but ask: Why do they do that? Why is there a pitched roof on it? Why are some of the rooms discrete? Why can we recognize it? Why does it look like a house if they're so intelligent?

JS: A modernist might say there's a lot of nostalgia in your work. And yet when they say they want to be more on the cutting edge, I think

Left: Maoli Residence, San Rafael.

Top and bottom: Maoli Residence, San Rafael.

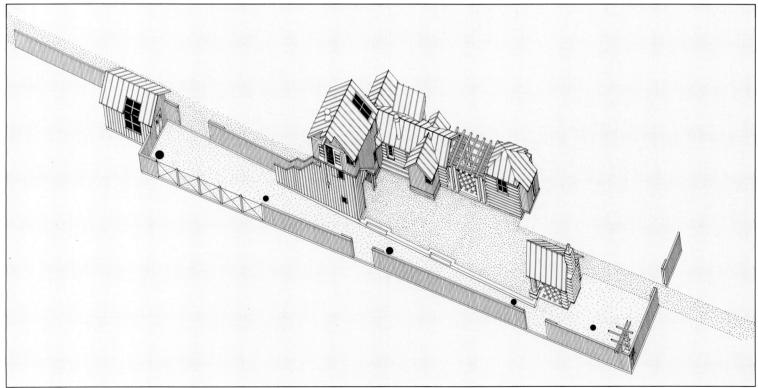

New Architecture

they're often expressing a deep nostalgia for the avant garde.

F&H: Absolutely. Deep nostalgia for the avant garde is a tremendous vanity. I think it's our consideration of what an appropriate gesture is, what the scale of a building is, and a sense of modesty that will determine whether we end up making some sort of impact on the architecture in this area. You don't have to stand up at the plate every time and go for a home run. The best work isn't always inspired by somebody who's trying to get published or die. A lot of the work I see now, which claims to be so avant garde and future-looking, is just frightened and arrogant and often totally egotistically driven. You need to constantly ask yourself, What is appropriate? At every point you have to keep that question in your mind. The result may veer toward being more traditional, or it may be more innovative. The important thing is that this intervention is what is appropriate here for these people in this location.

JS: A modernist that I interviewed for this book repeated the old argument from early modernist days that non-modernist work generally doesn't apply itself to global issues the way modernist work does. He thinks that modernist work has more of an applicability worldwide, in the way the International Style supposedly did, than nonmodernist work.

F&H: I think that criticism gets really reductive. It's a superficial kind of critique. Is the modernist work appropriate because it goes back to the 20s? A lot of the modern stuff we look at is from the 20s. What are those values? Do you do a painted wooden railing, or do you do a metal pipe railing? One is global and one isn't? Is that what it comes down to? You do a flat roof versus a pitched roof, and one is global and one isn't? Because the flat roof talks about the "modern condition of living" and the other one talks about the "old condition of living?" You know, some of it is so thin it's almost embarrassing to talk about as far as I'm concerned.

Intellectually, the modernist critique is the easier critique to make. You know, it's sort of avant-garde. But, the history of modernism came to a bad end. Architecture is being revitalized now, partially as a dialectical process of looking at what was missing historically. You hear a lot of voices trying to gloss over the fact that there is a correction, a dialectical shift, but I think architecture is revitalized for it.

JS: But, part of that shift, or correction, seems to have become an out-and-out aping of the past.

F&H: As part of the correction, architecture had to mimic tradition in order to learn it again. But, as a solution, you can't go for the Ralph Lauren look of total historicism. It's silly. We all know the world has changed a lot, and besides, that stuff costs a heck of a lot more now. The most important thing for us about the postmodern thing and the historical thing is a refocusing on where we are building. The International Style was rootless and placeless. We've all lost ground because of that.

Top left: Bailey Residence, Kentfield.

Bottom left: Berggruen Residence, Napa Valley.

Top and bottom: Berggruen Residence, Napa Valley.

I think it's silly to reduce the issue to something like the so-called forward-looking International Style versus the retrograde romantic. Much of the debate within the profession is carried on at that level. Good work is good work. So much of what gets talked about is only 10 percent of the job. In reality, good work sites a project, good work designs it, and good work assembles it. If global issues are a stylistic issue, then it's true that our architecture doesn't apply itself to global issues.

JS: Having visited the Berggruen House in the Napa Valley, I don't understand how you have so thoroughly been tarred with the brush of regionalism.

F&H: Because you don't think it's regionalist?

JS: Not in a Bay Area regionalist sense. Do you?

F&H: No. I think we see it as a Bay region house in the sense that it pays a lot of attention to the site.

Top, bottom, and facing page: Berggruen Residence, Napa Valley.

JS: Well, it is place-driven, as they say, and at the same time it's like a rural train station and a grain elevator, picturesque and camplike at the same time. These are all criteria of regionalist work in the area. Yet the house does not seem regionalist.

F&H: Well, it could easily not be specifically regionalist. If you set your goal to be a regionalist, I think it's a mistaken goal. Regionalism is more of a sensibility, not a style. I think a hidden premise of the recent show called "Radical Regionalism" at the San Francisco Arts Commission Gallery was that regionalism is a style. The show presented it pastiched together as a style composed of allusions and symbolism, saying that's what it is. But, I think the Bay regional style has nothing to do with that.

JS: What do you think it has to do with?

F&H: I think it has to do with a kind of understanding of the site-specific nature of things and how materials express what a building is. But it's more the physical quality of the place. Sometimes it's a connection to other issues, ways, and methods of building that have worked in an area. A lot has to do with a slight sort of arrogance of being on the edge of the world, or independence. Regionalism has always been antimovement, a kind of protest architecture, and I've always liked that. But, meaning it doesn't want to be somewhere else doesn't mean it wants to be picturesque and cute, a series of quotations. I think the best thing it has going for it is its stance as a protest architecture.

JS: And yet, the Berggruen House almost fits a check list of the so-called attributes of Bay region architecture: for example, the indoor-outdoor character of the plan development, the detailing of the exterior dining areas, and what I see as the miniaturized scale of the entire place. Does it seem miniature to you?

F&H: I would never call it miniature, because, to me, that's related to cuteness and sentimentality. The smallness of it, I think, is very radical. I think it relates to a side of us that is still interested in social issues and energy conservation. I think one of the good things about this area is that it retains some sort of more civilized consciousness about larger issues of environment. The house plays off that issue and the issue of appropriate size. For the Berggruen House, we had clients who weren't bloated with a kind of spatial gluttony. They were willing to ask What is it that we need? How big does this space need to be?

Designing this house was one of the most wonderful processes we've had with a client. The clients are both artists, so we could just talk with them about the design and be vulnerable. And their lifestyle isn't the usual. It was one of those special moments when someone comes with a life that's a little more richly expressed in ways we could understand. And a lot of the inspiration came from the site, from the Napa Valley, the towers in the valley. They were open to that.

JS: There are other attributes of the Bay region style that the building somehow seems to fit without succumbing to picturesque regionalism. Something that fits as a characteristic is the occasional use of something ugly, a building mass or shape, to give the entire composition more bite than it might otherwise have. I'm really struck by what I think is the ugliness of the stair to the studio glommed onto the tower. I'm not being critical of the building. It works very well. It seemed like you took something really ungainly, put it in just the right spot in the composition, and it worked very nicely.

F&H: I like the stair as well. We do architecture from the point of view of where we are. But, it's more the physical quality of the place. Sometimes it's a connection to other issues, ways, and methods of building that have worked in an area. I'm pleased that you think of it as a conundrum. I can't think of anything I'd rather have said about the work. It's your very ambiguous response to it that we want to get out of someone.

Likewise, it's encouraging that you're finding regionalism a hard thing to pinpoint. We actually view regionalism as an outsider's term. We understand regionalism to be an expression of "point of view" quite literally. Buildings, if they are to be constructed, have to be "somewhere." And that "somewhere" always carries the possibility of recognition, even if it is very abstract—like a machine part that can be traced to a particular model. Regionalism is a means, not an end.

Fisher-Friedman Associates

Robert Fisher, Rodney Friedman, and Robert Geering

 Since 1964 the firm of Fisher-Friedman Associates has acted as architect for nearly two hundred thousand units of housing in North America and Europe. The founders of the firm are Robert Fisher and Rodney Friedman. Their work has been exhibited at the Museum of Modern Art in New York and the San Francisco Museum of Modern Art. In addition to housing, they do excellent commercial work. With Fisher-Friedman Associates since its early days, Robert Geering has been instrumental in setting the firm's design attitudes.

JS: A year or two ago in *Atlantic* magazine I read an article on architecture in which you were extravagantly praised as doing "perhaps the best housing of this century."

FF: I don't know if the article said *century*, but we agree with them.

JS: Why did they say that?

FF: If you're looking at the firm from the outside in and depend on magazines for your information, you'll find that we've been published more than any other firm doing housing and have more awards for housing than any other firm in the nation. One of the reasons that our firm has done as well as it has is because we're always trying to step up a little higher. We're not going to do the kind of crackerbox stuff you see in housing tracts. What we're trying to do is enhance the housing element and make it better. When we started there weren't many architects who did work for developers. Most architects thought housing was dirty laundry, so in the early years there wasn't much competition. We came on board just as housing design was changing, at a time when housing was evolving into things like attached row and townhouses, garden patio apartments, and other ways of living different than normal tract housing.

JS: I want to ask you about the Golden Gateway project in San Francisco near the Ferry Building. Other architects with whom I've spoken have talked about designing housing projects for San Francisco that respect its typological patterns, such as the midblock alley and the courtyard house. Did the Golden Gateway incorporate any of that kind of thinking?

FF: Yes, but not by design only. I can take the mystique out of the design concept very simply: Our client at Alcoa said, "Let's divide the project into three blocks, because we can do it in phases that will be fundable and affordable." The Pacific Avenue Mall came out of that. The raised podium concept was the surviving element of an award-winning design by Wurster Bernardi and Emmons in 1960.

Above: Golden Gateway Commons, San Francisco.

Facing page top and bottom: Golden Gateway Commons, including site plan, San Francisco.

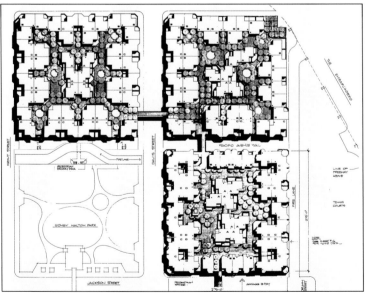

So, without getting mystical about this design, we picked up on the idea of the project working as lowrise, although we didn't know whether that meant four, five, or six stories, or whether it included commercial until we went through it empirically and did the number-crunching. After those parameters were established, which had to do with organizational ideas, the architecture started. It wasn't a case of following the neighborhood pattern, building typologies, or grid of the city. It didn't happen that way.

JS: Is that what you mean by the mystique?

FF: Yes. It was a very pragmatic way of making a community integrate. We thought of the typological considerations and so forth, but not to the point of writing essays about them. This project came about more through a visceral and empirical process. And it was the first of all the mixed-use projects. No question about it.

JS: To me, the mixed-use aspect of it makes it live. I know you have talked about the importance of designing buildings in cities so that the lower floors allow a lot of vitality. At the Monterey Design Conference in 1986 I heard you talk about it. As I remember, a well-known planner from a large San Francisco firm was making a speech about urban design. You stood up and told him, very dramatically and to wild applause, that his firm could have everything above the fourth floor to design, and that you would take care of the rest.

FF: The historian Charles Jencks had finished speaking when the planner got up to show his slides. The first one was San Francisco from the air, with the TransAmerica, the Bank of America, and 345 California Center sticking their tops through the clouds. I commented, "That's not the way the urban environment works. You guys can have everything above the bottom forty feet, because all you're interested in is the tops of buildings. We'll take the first four stories." I remember saying that there is a solution to the problem, which was to make everything type 5 one-hour [a code restriction limiting building height], for a couple of years. Everyone clapped, except Jencks, who said, "What is type 5 one-hour?" Because we don't get many highrises to do, we're concerned about the lower floors. We've discovered that Philip Johnson and those other stars really don't worry about the bottom.

JS: Are you limiting the architectural scale of your buildings out of any dislike of highrises?

FF: No. I remember, again, at that conference, Charles Jencks boasting about London and implying that Americans don't know enough about urban situations and environments, and that London is better because it doesn't have highrises. And I said, "The truth is, during nearly the entire time London was being created their architects couldn't build highrises if they wanted to. They built as high as they could out of stone. The only highrises they could build were churches." They put all the technology they had to get those buildings as tall as they could.

The message for us is that there is nothing really wrong with the heights of buildings. It's what you do with the bases of them. The thing we accuse our colleagues of forgetting is what happens at grade, laying waste to the ground plane and concentrating on the fancy tops of their buildings.

JS: At Golden Gateway why did you use brick?

FF: It was a memory from when we were working at Beckett's office in San Francisco years ago and had to go up to the produce district, where the project now is, to interview the food produce people about moving to a project that Beckett's office was working on. When we got the Golden Gateway project, we remembered the brick buildings in that neighborhood, the produce district. One might think that we would have chosen to tie the buildings visually to Wurster's housing, but we made a conscious decision to do something that tied the work more to the Jackson Square area and to complement what had been there in the past.

JS: The way you describe the development of the Golden Gateway project, the number-crunching and the phasing for funding, is exciting, but it is very seldom communicated or taught in architectural education. In reading the architectural press, a nonarchitect might think that the most important values of the profession are tied up in a desperate, ongoing beauty contest. How do you communicate what you've learned?

FF: One way our message gets out is in the form of publication in magazines such as *Housing*, which is a different kind of forum than *Progressive Architecture*. That's not to say we wouldn't like to be on the cover of *Domus*, though.

The important things we've learned have been learned empirically and intuitively. For example, we learned about money and projects through our desire to have things built. The project that doesn't get built and sits in the drawer doesn't do anybody any good. You probably have an angry client or a client that's out of business. You don't get published, you don't get a repeat client, and you don't get any business from that project through other potential clients seeing it. Projects have to make a statement and work well for people, but they also have to be built. That's what leads into the financial feasibility and the costing we do. We want to get every project built.

Also, in school we are trained to design a project, render it very handsomely, and try to sell it to a jury of professors. That's not the way the real world works, at least in housing. You have to work in your shirt sleeves beside your client as a cooperative or team. You have to have that involvement and cooperation from the very beginning.

There is plenty of room for art. Many developers have become much more sophisticated. I remember in the 60s if you mentioned the word *award* to a client they would shudder and say, We don't want any awards, just a successful project. Now they all say, When are we going to get our award, when are we going to be pub-

lished? Now they realize you can do good projects and make money and still have the art and the award.

JS: Doing such a volume of housing, how do you keep your work fresh?

FF: We are always looking for a new way to do a project, to the point of frustration for some people in the office. We don't do "drawer jobs," even though they are easier.

JS: A couple of years ago I saw a very innovative project by an architect named Ted Smith in San Diego that allowed the buyers to lay out their units. Each unit was a shell with a kit of parts from which the buyers put together their units through the arrangement of modules containing parts of the home. Have you ever done anything like that?

FF: We did work in Holland in 1978 that included discussion with the client about doing units that were shells the client could modify to suit, but it never actually happened. We are now working on a job with a very, very schematic design of loft-type units that would be marketed as

shells. The shell would be a two-story space, 18 feet wide and 18 feet high, or something like that, with a menu or kit of parts people could use to create their own spaces.

JS: What do you do besides housing?

FF: We did the Vintage Country Club project, near Palm Springs, and we are doing many office buildings. We're trying to break out of this stereotype of only doing what some people think of as developer housing. We're not getting away from housing, though, just expanding in other directions. No one associates us with that kind of work. But we do it very well.

Above: South Beach Marina, San Francisco.

James Gillam Architects

James Gillam

 After traveling throughout the world and receiving a Graduate Diploma in Architecture from The Architectural Association in London, England, James Gillam established his practice as an architect in 1976. His varied practice includes residential and commercial work. His Yardley/Porter Residence in Guerneville, California, received a Progressive Architecture Award in 1982.

JS: A complaint about modern architecture is that its so-called abstraction makes it impossible for people to relate to it. I don't think that's a problem with your Corte Madera office building. To me it's a building that is very evocative through its abstract forms. It's almost nautical, without any overt references to the sea. It relates beautifully to its site on San Francisco Bay.

JG: There are allusions in this project to its relationship to the Bay, the water, the mud, and the fill on which the building rests. I dwelled on those things a lot in my sketchbooks during its design. I've always seen the building as a kind of broken hull.

JS: That has washed up in the mud?

JG: It's washed up, in a similar way to how one used to occasionally see ferryboats in Sausalito washed up in the mud. So, it's somewhat boat-like, and some of the detailing is rather nautical. There are also the relationships it has with the wind and the sun in terms of energy conservation. Beyond that, and the proportions and articulation, is a careful study of alignments and cost-effective materials.

JS: With regard, though, to the general form, or even pattern of the building, it seems to have a primitivist cast to it in the way the parapets are detailed.

JG: Yes. I wanted to do something that was very simple on the one hand and a bit provocative on the other. The pattern of the building, which is a kind of step language that culminates in the parapet detailing, grew out of the fact that we had to fill the site to build on it. The building steps from the fill, to the concrete block, to the stucco frame, and to the wood apertures on the exterior. It was a very simple and inexpensive vocabulary to work with.

I also didn't want to differentiate too much between what most people consider landscape architecture and what others would consider architecture, or to have the landscape architecture considered as just residual space around the building. The site was too tight, and I wanted the two to merge. What has happened is that all of the planting, which has taken over and is now trailing from retaining walls, is now climbing the columns and growing all over the apertures, and the building is slowly but surely becoming a nonbuilding.

JS: How did the building get so stretched out and segmented?

JG: The shape of the site, which is 115 feet wide and 360 feet deep, limits you to doing either some sort of stretched out linear scheme such as this or doing a condensed version at the back of the site, with parking facilities at the front. Also, the site is in a flood plain, and because of long-term differential settlement, it was recommended that the massing be divided into smaller buildings. Thus, we really have four separate buildings ledgered together. Also, this was designed as an office condominium project, with the intent of selling off portions of the building. This required parking and immediate access to as many of the units as possible. The other reason for stretching it out was to create a building that was as energy-passive as possible. To accomplish that we gave every office a northern and southern exposure.

JS: I like the building's circulation space being all outside.

JG: I did it because of the Bay Area climate and the energy considerations and because exterior corridors and balconies were exempted from the gross allowable building area. As it was, we had a terrible time getting this building approved. The architecture is very unpopular with the planning commission.

JS: It is?

JG: Yeah. It was nearly rejected, or overridden, by the town council and the planning committee after it was unanimously and wholeheartedly approved by the design review board.

JS: Why?

JG: It's in a strange location, one that has never been tested in terms of proper usage. It's zoned for limited commercial and light industrial.

JS: Your work has a very appealing reductive nature to it.

JG: A theoretical basis for my work is simplicity. I've always loved minimalism. I think that love always underwrites my thinking and the search for an ideal minimalist space. To me, minimalist detailing is very rich—the way light hits something, what happens between, say, a tree and a building, or what color and materials can mean in a minimalist kind of sense.

This approach produces buildings that are very serene and very refreshing and peaceful. This isn't to say, though, that minimalism as a type of expressiveness is going to solve planning problems and other large issues. But, you have to design spaces and minimalist spaces of varying scale perform as well as anything that has been done. As an architect, I'm not sure I'd call myself strictly a minimalist. In architecture, in contrast to art, the scale of the problem is generally such that you find yourself working

with the people who are going to build your building, or live in it, or whatever. That sets up a different dynamic in the way a project comes together beyond one's own specific kind of design approach.

JS: There are other architects in the Bay Area who feel in some ways the way you do. In their work you also see a paring down, a reduction of elements, and an elimination of what they and you regard as the nonessentials of architecture.

JG: I think there is a fascination with materials specific to this area's resources, as well as a particular understanding of the land and climate of California, that combine to create a regional aspect to what I suppose you could call regional architecture. There are things you can do in northern California that you couldn't get away with in other climates that involve the environmental aspect, as well as the use of materials and ways of designing buildings to resist earthquakes.

JS: If you were to summarize your concerns in architecture, what would you say?

JG: I've gone back and forth over the last twenty years liking many different things. The things I always come back to and love and appreciate the most are simple, and therefore I think more valuable.

Top: office building, Corte Madera.
Bottom: Yardley/Porter Residence, Guerneville.

Holt Hinshaw Pfau Jones Architecture

Peter Pfau and Wes Jones

Recently honored with a Progressive Architecture Award for their Astronauts Memorial design, a commission it secured by winning a national competition, the firm of Holt Hinshaw Pfau Jones practices architecture seldom surpassed for its use and expression of contemporary technology in buildings. Established in 1981 and based in San Francisco's North Beach, the firm has a staff of twenty-five and a Los Angeles branch office. The four partners, Paul Holt, Marc Hinshaw, Peter Pfau, and Wes Jones take pride not only in their award-winning designs, but also in their ability through aggressive business skills to secure a wide range of commissions.

JS: What did the ad agency cost?

HHPJ: It's cheap, dirt cheap. I mean, it's $15 per square foot, so cheap it's disgusting.

JS: What kind of client lets you do this?

HHPJ: They're quite ideal in some ways. On one level they don't have much money, which is not ideal, but they are very creative people and were open to a creative exchange with us. We really did have fun making architecture for them. They are a very avant garde ad agency and wanted architecture that would be as weird as they are.

JS: What else was on your mind when you did this?

HHPJ: There is a little bit of the idea of collage or fragmentation. In other words, a thing has landed in the corridor and goes up through the ceiling and down through the floor in some kind of collage-of-reality condition. There is the sense that the architecture was something they could fiddle with and change.

JS: You like things that move in buildings, don't you?

HHPJ: Yes, a lot of people focus on that. It's not an end in itself, but it does create a level of engagement. It ties in perfectly with the whole mechanical rap we are trying to espouse. It also gives more visual interest to the building because of the language of the things that make the parts work. In the case of the segmented garage doors, we had to do a whole lot of head scratching because we were trying to do things with them that you don't normally do. Here they serve as a slash between public and private space. Obviously, it is not complete visual and acoustic privacy, but it does give a sense of enclosure while at the same time being able to open up the office as a whole for some kind of large open house. You definitely get the reading that there are a bunch of reasonably banal walls and so forth into which this thing has been inserted. You are engaged because of your interaction with it on all sides as you move around it.

Left and Right: Altman and Manley Advertising Agency, San Francisco.

JS: How about the Right Away Ready Mix cement batching plant for which you received a design award. At what stage is it?

HHPJ: It is in the city permit process now. You have to understand that it's so small it will take three months to build.

JS: What happened? I remember the project being quite large.

HHPJ: It was an involved permitting process. By the time it was finished, the clients had grown out of the project. It's a drag, because we have a lot invested in the old building and had finished working drawings, which were very laboriously detailed. So we are looking for anyone who would like a totally designed, contract documents completed, award-winning concrete batching plant for the cost of construction management only and the cost of the prints.

JS: For whom did you do the suburban house?

HHPJ: A contemporary of ours who grew up with Pete, and whom we would call an enlightened developer. This design is really a critical piece, a reaction to the trend within normal, already built-up suburbs.

JS: I hope you build it. There is a criticism of "techy" houses that they don't seem very homey or livable. I've been in some in Los Angeles and they are quite wonderful inside.

HHPJ: This house in particular is trying to be engaging or homey in the way a sailboat can be, a cruising sailboat that has the same interactive condition with the environment and with day-to-day experience.

JS: What are the things that make that happen?

HHPJ: At the most obvious, overt level, there is a lot of stuff that moves, through which you can enlarge or shrink spaces, condition the sunlight that enters, get places where you can't get otherwise, and that sort of thing. That's the most obvious level. But there is also an attempt to make somewhat treehouse-like spaces that give the sense of security Wright achieved.

JS: Your architecture strongly celebrates technology, much more than almost any other work being done today.

HHPJ: We feel very strongly that technology is the essence of now, that there is a technological state we have all progressed to and are dependent upon. The presence of the machine and the mechanical metaphor in our understanding of the world is undeniable. We are trying to understand technology, and trying, through a rigorous analysis, to understand what it is that architecture today should express. We keep coming back to this idea of mechanism in the very broadest sense, which is really just that thing which man makes. Everything you try to explain gets explained in some veiled way or another in terms of some kind of what we can only call mechanical analogy, whether it is thought or language or art.

JS: Either in the talk in your studio or in your writing, how do you discuss the abstract elements of architecture such as the meanings of line or mass or void?

HHPJ: We try very hard not to talk about architectural things in the language we were all trained to talk about them with—it has a lot to do with not limiting the results. We came from an age when foamcore board and axis were the two strongest form determinants in architecture. We felt strongly that there had to be much more interesting ways. In the studio, which is where everything happens, we communicate to our draftsmen in much more of a coded language. We tend to work here saying things like, Couldn't you just tweak that a little, or add more flipper over here.

JS: In trying to understand your work I've read some of your writings. In this article, "Building Machines," which was in *Pamphlet Architecture #12*, I found a number of succinct statements in the captions under photographs and drawings. For example, "The machine is not an agent of alienation to be feared. As a definitive product of his will it is the signifier for man." Rather than publish an interview with you in the book, I could list your sayings and aphorisms.

HHPJ: A lot of avant garde or revolutionary architecture is presented in little aphorisms. We don't consider ourselves avant garde. Rather than present ourselves that way, what we want to present are fully argued, fully reasoned propositions. It's a little dangerous to just sort of list a group of axioms on one page, because then it will appear that we are just a bunch of futurist jerks. We are trying to be a little more reasonable than that.

JS: So, having carefully constructed your thoughts, you have an architectural philosophy that is based on sound reason and rationality. Correct?

HHPJ: To the extent that anything can be based on reason. In other words, now that we've been back East and tasted post-structuralism and have all this magic self-awareness the structuralists themselves apparently did not have, we have a sense of irony. It's hard for us to make a bald statement that the world is reasonable or that one can get anywhere by reason. We are trying to come up with an architecture that could be rationally explained rather than just the this-is-my-kind-of-stuff routine. It's not reason but rigor that can take you to a certain point. Then you have to look at it and judge whether it's worthwhile. Beyond the system, there is your intuition.

At a certain point you have to go beyond the tools you used to get there. But, then again, as any post-structuralist would quibble, you have to be able to subject the leap of intuition to a check, which again is reason and rigor. The people we are usually allied with are people we find to be a bit more personal and a bit more art oriented, style oriented than we are. Essentially, we are trying to create a vernacular for the next five hundred years.

JS: That's quite an ambition.

HHPJ: Architecture is, or was, the biggest thing that man did. For the stuff to be strong enough to last, it has to have that strength of desire.

JS: You are influenced strongly, it seems, by the post-structuralist thinking you encountered in New York and perhaps by deconstructivism as well. Do you think that when we as architects study our art our time is well spent pondering in such great detail attitudes based in contemporary literary theory? Do you think design professionals are going in meaningful directions?

HHPJ: The whole starting point of linguistics that tracks through a gross misunderstanding in postmodernism and informs a lot of work going on now is unquestionably important. And, if you go back to defining intangibles like architecture today, one of the most basic assumptions in any definition of architecture is that it expresses something about the society for which it is built, something about its highest aspirations and ideals. Where there is nothing to glorify, there can be no architecture. The post-structuralist thing is really a good window on the way we view the world today. To the extent that architecture as architecture is seen this way, you must take into account the latest view of society.

JS: I recently read an article in *The New Criterion* by Diana Ketcham in which she talks about how Frank Gehry's work contains a sense of cultural despair. She questions whether buildings ought to express doubt and evanescence. It's fascinating to correlate building forms with the spirit of an age.

HHPJ: If you're an architect who really cares, you have to have some direction. There is none now. I'm not sure Gehry is onto a direction so much as a criticism. Our work isn't critical, except to the extent it's different. It's intended to evoke a world where it would be the norm;

whereas, my sense is that the work of the other architects like Gehry is based on critique. This is the age of critique.

JS: Considering the amount of time you've practiced, you've written a great deal, voluminously it seems, about why you do what you do. Why, and who reads it?

HHPJ: Well, we do it for ourselves as much as for anybody else, to keep track of what we're doing and to check to make sure we are straight. We call it the equation.

JS: Your desire to create such a lasting vernacular perhaps requires a text to go along with the actual work.

HHPJ: Yes and no. Ideally, in the final analysis the object would be read by itself and wouldn't require a text.

JS: I think that's true. but look at Wright or Le Corbusier, for example. Their writings greatly helped spread their ideas as their work began to take hold. In the short haul. . . .

HHPJ: In the short haul, you find yourself in a situation where somebody will say, Well, it feels right, but I can't figure out why, because it's so weird, or something like that. It's nice to pull out the text then, or to be able to explain to a person that it feels right for all the appropriate reasons. Essentially, the project-specific text comes after, but the general ones are really more parallel investigations.

We are trained to think of architectural thought as having a direct connection between what, for example, Aldo Rossi writes and what Aldo Rossi does. If you really look closely you realize there is a great disjunction—and we admit that disjunction. We admit that when we work a lot of the work is intuitive, but the basis of our intuition is a very rigorous development of our thought about how we are going to work. Since our major design tool is intuition, we try to hone it, to further educate and refine it.

The species of thought that has been codified in structural and post-structural thinking is a visual kind, where the metaphors like collage or graft or disjunction have direct visual application. Somebody like Eisenman or Zaha Hadid or another deconstructivist has tools that came directly out of the vocabulary that the post-structuralists used, tools that have an immediate visual application. It is more difficult, I think, when you are dealing with a figural world, as we are in our work, than when you work within an abstract world like the others I mentioned. For example, we have to justify a landing flap as an appropriate reference, because it has no direct grammatical linkage to the words you are dealing with. In other words, you can say the thing should move, but why it should move in this particular way is a much harder thing to translate. The philosophy is a philosophy of manipulation given a figure. It is the grammar that tells you how to manipulate the figure to make a visible rhetoric. The kinds of argumentative, philosophical, or rhetorical figures that work in language and speech and philosophy can be translated directly. They are all syntactical things without a semantic content and are all questions of manipulation or activity upon something. You have to figure out what "thing" is appropriate to start with. That is where we try to focus.

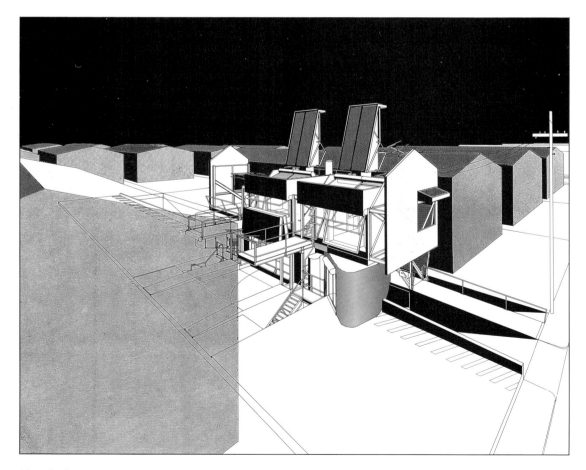

Left: suburban house.

I.O.O.A.
Interim Office of Architecture
John Randolph and Bruce Tomb

 John Randolph and Bruce Tomb are partners in the firm I.O.O.A., the Interim Office of Architecture, in San Francisco. They met as architecture students at California Polytechnic University in San Luis Obispo. Tomb and Randolph established I.O.O.A. in 1984 to encourage collaborations between architects and artists on a variety of design projects, which include furnishings, interiors, and buildings. The I.O.O.A.'s collaborative efforts in furniture design have been extensively published, and Bruce Tomb's "granite cooktop" was exhibited in the Whitney Museum's exhibit, "High Styles," in 1985.

JS: The bathroom renovation you did for the Headlands project in Marin County looks like where I would go to clean up after a hard day of driving my Dodge Ramcharger across a desert in Australia. Why do your projects look like sets for Road Warrior movies?

IOOA: A lot of people pick up on that. We don't see them that way. We're not nihilists. Nihilism often goes hand-in-hand with pessimism. We like a quote of Roberto Rossellini's: "I am not a pessimist. To perceive evil where it exists is, in my opinion, a form of optimism."

JS: It's just that a lot of your work looks apocalyptic. What are you trying to do here?

IOOA: A little background of the project would be helpful to you. The project is for the Headlands Center for the Arts. They've taken the building over from the park service, who has taken it over from the military. They commission artists to do permanent installations, which are both historical renovations and contemporary art projects. David Ireland is the first artist employed on the project, and he set the tone for the whole place. In his work at Headlands he acknowledged what was there and altered it sensitively, in an archeological sense. That attitude had a big impact on the aesthetic of our project, especially the walls and surfaces. Our project was to renovate a latrine for use by men and women at the same time.

JS: So the space is entirely still functioning?

IOOA: Only in part. The latrine has a row of urinals that were vandalized and in disrepair. We decided to leave them dysfunctional to emphasize them as relics, as well as to negate their original "male-specific" function. In the middle of the room there were ten toilets. We eliminated two of them for exiting and handicap access. Six toilets were partitioned for basic individual privacy. Two toilets were plumbed, but left exposed, and they now serve as icons for the space and an alternative for the bold or desperate.

JS: Did you have any desire to warm up the space?

IOOA: Not from the standpoint of bringing in any mechanical aspect into it, or carpeting, because we wanted to keep the original character of the latrine in its starkness, and actually amplify some of the coldness, while muting it by introducing a feminine aspect.

JS: What would you say that is?

IOOA: The feminine aspect of our work surfaces in two different ways. The first and most schematic is the overall layout, which develops a stronger symmetry in the space, which implies a similarity between sexes as opposed to sameness. The second feminine aspect to the project is the duality of approaches taken towards the detailing of the space. This may be seen in the contrast of the delicate technique we employed to strip the paint off the walls contrasted with the boldness of the toilet stalls, which, again, form a protective enclosure around the fragile porcelain toilets.

JS: The showers are still used?

IOOA: They are, primarily by the few people in residence there. The Headlands doesn't need a lot of shower space at this time. Part of the area is set up as dressing areas with teak benches and flooring. That was an area where we introduced another material warm to the touch, in contrast to the existing galvanized partitions.

JS: Why was it important to expose the workings of the plumbing?

IOOA: Basically, it's to become more aware of the systems that are inherent in this kind of space so there is a sense of the space as a room with the utilities running through it. We went to great efforts to magnify or accentuate any possibility of noise or movement created by the water.

JS: What are the plan concepts?

IOOA: By looking at the diagram of the plan of the stalls, you can see that the space is organized not unlike the human body. It's an anthropomorphic layout with a big pair of iron lungs, a spine, and even a crotch piece. The stalls plan is superimposed over an extremely accurate field measure drawing of what is built, which is in turn superimposed over an enlarged original military drawing for the space. The two vaguely correspond, illustrating discrepancy.

JS: So?

IOOA: It emphasizes the contradictions inherent in the military institution. Things start off wanting to be a certain way but don't end up that way. We played off the idea of how the military has changed. We dealt with the ideas of what is excessive.

JS: So, the quarter-inch steel toilet partitions are a comment on the military's enormous budget?

Left: bathroom, Headlands Center for the Arts, Marin County.

IOOA: Sure. But, it also deals with our culture's ideas of privacy. You can go to all this trouble to develop systems of privacy for yourself in your life, using very substantial things. But, if you go into this space, it's quite apparent you have no privacy.

JS: At the same time, though, there is this almost brutal kind of protection of your body from physical attack.

IOOA: It seems like that, but the aspect of privacy that is most immediate and probably most important for this space, visual privacy, is scantily addressed. Partitions are higher up off the floor than normal and lower from the ceiling than normal. It's the absolute minimum we could get away with before people would be too paranoid to use the space.

I want to mention another idea in the plan. The space is bisected into two halves, although there is no designation for male and female. We alluded to the sexes in the shapes of the toilet stalls. One shape is more rectilinear, rational, and sharp. The other is more irrational and curvilinear, and more responsive to site conditions.

JS: Aren't you propagating stereotypes?

IOOA: No, I don't think so. We're investigating archetypes. There is no sign saying that one stall is for women and another for men. It's up to the user to pick the one he or she wants.

JS: I think I'd feel like a general in the largest stall.

IOOA: Yes, it's great. On the other hand we have the smallest one, which is very interesting, because it's the absolute minimum you can get away with. Your knees hit the door when you sit down.

JS: There are men and women in here at the same time?

IOOA: Yes, there are. There are also men and women showering at the same time. The wedge plan shape has two doors that swing open, with one side for men and one for women, but it's not specific. Because it's not designated, the men's and women's sides can be mixed up, although there are social mores saying you shouldn't mix them. That's where our society and its toilet training come into the situation. Basically, people are allowed to use this space in any way they want to.

JS: Don't you think a more specific gender separation is a good idea? Is it all right, for example, to have young girls showering with older men?

IOOA: And young boys showering with older women? The separation will monitor itself.

JS: So, rather than put the decision in the hands of the institution, you put it in the hands of the individuals.

IOOA: It's their decision. Children would probably be in the space with a parent. You could design yourself blue in the face and it still won't change what a child will naively do. The design of a bathroom can be one of the most significant design problems. It contains so many charged issues that may be universal. What we tried to work with was the idea of men and women using the space together, without favoring one over the other.

JS: How do people like using this place?

IOOA: We've gotten mixed comments. I received a comment from somebody who thought that it was the greatest imposition on humanity they'd ever experienced. Generally, the comments are much more complimentary. People love it and find the space and its ideas amusing, exciting, and provocative.

Facing page top and bottom: bathroom, Headlands Center for the Arts, Marin County.

Right: bathroom, Headlands Center for the Arts, Marin County.

Jim Jennings Arkhitekture

Jim Jennings

 The modernist architecture of Jim Jennings has been published widely in America and Europe. Formerly in partnership with William Stout and now practicing individually, Jennings brings to his work a fine level of detail, most recently seen in his work with steel. He has taught at University of California, Berkeley and the California College of Arts and Crafts, and lectured to AIA chapters and at various schools. Among his current projects are private residences in the East Bay and Stinson Beach, banks, and additions and renovations to hospitals.

Above: World Savings
Headquarters, Oakland.

JS: Your World Savings project derives some of its elegance from a design attitude that is in part somewhat minimalist and reductivist. I want to read you a quote from Vincent Scully's recent article, "Le Corbusier, 1922–1965," in *Le Corbusier*, edited by H. Allen Brooks, and ask you to apply it to your work as an architect.

Left and below: World Savings
Headquarters, Oakland.

Does, for example, the elimination of almost all directly associational and most purely plastic detail that his [Corbusier's] buildings of the twenties shared with those of De Stijl, Gropius, Mies, and so many others constitute in fact a serious reduction rather than a liberation of architecture's vocabulary? Does the so-called Modern Movement, or rather that specific part of modern architecture that Hitchcock and Johnson called the International Style, represent, despite the many acknowledged masterpieces that it produced, a temporary and, as seen at this moment in time, almost inconceivable aberration in the general development of architectural tradition and of modern architecture as a whole? Does not such reductiveness, if it should indeed be regarded as that, represent a romantic primitivism that is hard to square with the complex urbanistic traditions that have in fact formed modern cities and, indeed, all types of contemporary buildings?

JJ: I was thinking as you were talking about the whole idea of reduction being seen as against something. To me, Scully is saying that to be reductivist in your aesthetic attitude is to negate something. I don't look at it that way. I see it more as a beginning from nothing and making something—more as a manifesto against ornament, or against tradition, or against the classical or the postmodern. It's much more direct. There are two things about World Savings that are important to me with regard to what you just said. One is that when certain things were done there was a reason for doing them. First of all there might have been a functional requirement, or there might have been a visual requirement, things that had to be done in a certain way, which my clients and I could agree on. Beyond that, there's the doing of it, the making of it, which is where it gets interesting to me.

JS: But now it sounds like there may be a very functionalist bias in your approach to architecture, perhaps the kind of thinking that postmodernism was trying to change.

JJ: I don't think so. Everything that's done in architecture having its beginning in some rational basis doesn't have to be functionalist. Someone doesn't have to be labeled a functionalist because he begins with rationality. We're rational beings, and architecture, because of its complexity, requires rationality. And because there's a reason for something to be done doesn't mean that there is a reason for it to be done one particular way. At some point the rational part of your thinking stops and something else takes over. For example, why did you put a curve in the street façade of the house you're designing now in the upper Haight? It's because at some point something else took over that had nothing to do with the fact that you needed a façade for the building. I think the crux of the question has to do with what architecture is, because it is a rational art. But it's also an intuitive art. It's a social art, and it's a perceptual and psychological art.

JS: Where do you fall in that range?

JJ: Probably in several categories, except the social. For example, my house in Lafayette was in some respects based on ideas I had years ago which came from Jung's writings about his own house. There is something that touched me in reading his description of how he came up with the idea of four pavilions to live in as his home evolved and how each of the pavilions had its own meaning. Once the idea was there for me it was intrinsic in the organization the same way a more strictly functional requirement would be. These thoughts were part of the basis for the house's organization but not factors in how it's made. As I said with regard to World Savings, I've become very fascinated in recent years with just the making of things. On three different projects currently we're designing all of the window and door sections, even those that could be taken for granted or pulled from a catalog, which is a dangerous thing for architects to do, but very important.

JS: Perhaps you can relate that to another quote from Scully about the character of space Le Corbusier created:

> It was Le Corbusier, in 1922, who suddenly exploited his new vision and architecturally endowed it with special dramatic aura that was to enable it to dominate the architectural world. The interior of his Ozenfant house literally explodes into space; all the old details of the great European tradition, which had qualified edges and modified changes of plane, are burned away by the whiteness of the light. All planes are as thin as paper, all frames are as taut as lines. High up in space one plane curves alone,

modeling the white light. Whatever the mechanism by which the architect was seeing, he was clearly doing so with an excitement about flatness, thinness, light, and an elimination of detail that had never been so passionately felt by any architect.

JJ: That, to me, is a beautiful description of somebody who got carried away by the excitement of making something. You know, though, there is something else in that quotation that strikes me as being really important, and forgotten in architecture, or at least presently lost—the experiential aspect of architecture, which Scully beautifully describes. I think the whole postmodern thing was image-related and had more to do with the image of space than the experience of it. It became a perfect expression of the 80s because it was so tied up in image.

JS: You excluded social concerns from your range of concerns in architecture. Many of the innovations of modernism in building, in housing in particular, grew out of technical and aesthetic concerns as well as any social agenda.

JJ: Sure. Modernism is blamed for sins it never committed. I think even the projects that had a so-called social basis, such as Corbu's Marseilles Block, really began as almost aesthetic projects. It was as though technology provided an aesthetic opportunity out of which he created something, rather than out of a social agenda. And other people did, too, although not nearly as well. It's incredible to me the buildings and projects he gets blamed for that he never designed. It's as if he designed the South Bronx, which the attackers of modernism say when they promote their back-to-the-past ideas. The problem in dealing with social concerns is to try to determine what they are. It's done very superficially, the same way attitudes about the use of history are generally applied to architecture.

JS: I recently spoke with Donald MacDonald, who builds a lot of very low-cost housing. He spoke about the problems of producing low-cost housing, and how a variety of things, from site acquisition to stair detailing, can swing the cost of a building many thousands of dollars.

JJ: If you translate that into a perceptual or visual approach to design, or the making of a wall or a door, you can be concerned about how the light falls on a certain wall, or what shape the wall is, or how it relates to the space it's in. MacDonald's concerns can become perceptual and visual.

JS: A criticism of modernism is that it ignores the past too much. In fact, isn't there a large legacy from the past in modern architecture?

JJ: Absolutely. I don't overtly refer to certain works, or certain buildings, but a respect for and a learning from the past is definitely there. If you have a respect for the examples of the past, you have a strength to begin with. Perhaps there is no direct reference to, say, Karl Schinkel's Altes museum sited next to a river, or whatever. Yet the power with which that building sits on its

Top and bottom: Group One, San Francisco.

site with relation to the river may influence you regarding relating a building to a space, or to water, for instance, or an edge.

JS: Or, even the rhythm of columns or fenestration. Robert Stern attacks modernism in "Pride of Place" when he says about the time of his student days when the postwar world was gone and modernism was triumphant that "I was reminded that just as I must learn to love the bomb, or at least live with it, I must learn to love an architecture that exalted function and structural technique as they are determinants of significant form." Here we have modern architecture connected to the atomic bomb, and elsewhere to the failure of the cities and the general failure of technology.

JJ: I don't know if it's because of the bomb, or a general lack of faith to solve our problems, or whatever, but I think it's natural for people who feel very frightened and uncertain to turn away from the future and from the outside world and look to the past for solace and to make the world more understandable. There really is a loss of faith in the external world. Creating a technology that enables buildings to look old by carefully restoring them, rather than renovating and updating them, or parodying them, treats the past with respect. Borrowing from the past essentially devalues it.

JS: It's our responsibility as architects and planners to help create buildings and cities that provide comfort and continuity. How that's done touches our deepest beliefs about who we are. In "Pride of Place" the last sequence was of Robert Stern and Leon Krier riding through Williamsburg, Virginia, extolling its virtues and saying that, in many ways, it represents what American architecture and cities should strive to be. Although they weren't calling for a verbatim recreation of Williamsburg, the effect was very odd, and almost chilling.

JJ: Williamsburg is a very nice prison camp, a detention camp full of people living comfortably in their knickers and buckle shoes, while they make candles. It doesn't have anything to do with real social concerns. It makes sense as a museum or as a cultural mausoleum. But to infer present or future realities from that situation can be no more than a coincidence. Trips to the past are no remedy. They help create a reduction to a low level of mediocrity and a homogenizing of our culture. This reminds me of *Howl*, Allen Ginsberg's poem of frustration and despair.

JS: As you said earlier, though, there is much to be learned from the spirit of the past.

JJ: I recently heard Frank Gehry and Cesar Pelli in a discussion moderated by Pilar Viladas in Los Angeles. She asked Pelli why his work doesn't have more references to the past. I liked his reply, which was something like, "I was born in the twentieth century and relate to my contemporaries. As a marvelous piece of architecture, I admire the Duomo in Florence. But I was not a contemporary of Brunelleschi. His clients weren't my clients and his technology is not my technology. Brunelleschi's building types were not my building types, nor is his culture mine. How can I relate to Brunelleschi?" That's not to say past cultures aren't important. Architecture is a critical trace of human energy and activity representative of all cultures. But the past is past. I think duplicating it is hopelessly out of touch with the world, and I think it's very pessimistic.

Rather than editorializing the past, I think we as architects and thinking human beings can help create a future that represents the highest ideals of our culture, not only as an image, but as reality. We should strive for that.

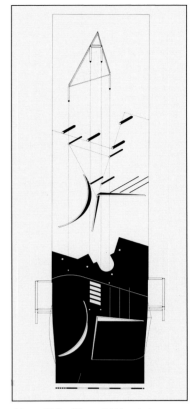

Above: Valley Memorial Hospital entrance canopy, Livermore.

Left: Pediatric Rehabilitation Unit; Children's Hospital, Oakland.

Hanns Kainz & Associates

Hanns Kainz

A native of Vienna, Austria, Hanns Kainz holds architecture and engineering degrees from the Technological University of Vienna, University of California, Berkeley, and Stanford University. He began his practice in 1978. Characterized by wit, elegance, and a great sensitivity to detailing, his work includes a large number of projects done for the garment business in the Bay Area and Los Angeles. His remodel of the Hamms Brewery building into a food service trade center is a prominent feature of San Francisco's Mission District. Hanns Kainz also designs furniture, and his Presidio chair, a construction of steel tubing and green khaki was a highlight of the 1987 Outdoor Chair Show curated by Tofer Delaney.

JS: What is the setting for the South of Market Jessica McClintock headquarters?

HK: It is a rehab of an art deco building built in 1938. The new entryway on this project appears to contain a lot of ideas but actually is very simple. To design it I took the space and consciously created three complications to work to.

JS: What were they?

HK: The first complication was to turn the entry lobby because I like to toy with people's curiosities. I turned it off what you would normally expect to be a symmetrical layout and located the symmetry in a different axis related to the mirror at the end of the space. So, when a person entering the space arrives at the mirror they encounter a surprise. Normally, in stairs designed similarly, as you find in the baroque, for example, when a person arrives at the same point they are frustrated, given the choice of turning left or right, either of which is identical. They have to make a decision and don't know what to base it on. That's why I changed it. You would think people would make a left turn at this point, now that the axis is turned, but some of them still go right. They must have a good reason. We'll probably never find out.

JS: What was the second complication you set for yourself?

HK: It was to create a streamline motif that would start somewhere at the bottom of the entryway and end up somewhere at the top, following the person ascending the stair and creating points of interest. The starting and ending points were arbitrary, although I wanted the motif to end somewhere near the client's offices. Extending this streamline motif up through the entryway tower created a number of complications. For example, I ran into a column, which is actually behind the wall but which I pulled forward to increase complications. You see, the real column is behind the fake one.

JS: The streamline motif could have risen directly up the stairway, but because there was a column in the wall you pulled it forward to interrupt the motif?

HK: Correct. But, I wasn't satisfied with its appearance, and had to work on it. I believe very much in the main elements of architecture: the door, the window, the stairs, the column. So, whenever I can I like to hit them. The window itself was there and I didn't feel the need to work on it, because its embellishment was created by bisecting it with the streamline motif, making it a negative and a positive. I thought it was just the appropriate scale.

JS: What was complication three?

HK: To introduce lines in the mirror itself, which then would intersect other lines in the space. They create joinery for the mirror, which is fairly large. The lines go up, they symbolize hope. They go upwards like statistics for the client. It gives you an "up" feeling. I don't like to talk about the practical aspects of it, but it was necessary to put the lines on the mirror because this stair is a main exit out of the building, and I don't want people running down the stairs and into the mirror. I was very intrigued about how to detail the mirror. The philosophy here is that the mirrors overlay. That's how I get the distortion. In between them is aluminum coming out, because the usual backing of silver would, in reality, run just under the glass.

JS: Whenever I'm in the neighborhood I look in the Jessica McClintock store on Sutter Street. It's a delightful design, and I want to ask you

Left and right: Jessica McClintock Headquarters, San Francisco.

about it. First of all, how did you come up with the neoclassic façade?

HK: In one sense, it's contextual. The store is located up the street from the Willis Polk Hallidie building, which has the cast-iron ornamentation in front of the glass, so that the glass curtain is entirely independent of the ornamentation. This you will find at the McClintock store.

The other influence on the façade was the idea that when an architect works for a retailer he finds himself doing a certain amount of advertising. In other words, he is creating a logo for the store, a logo that possibly can be carried on the shopping bags, for example, something that should be recognizable from a distance, to draw people, and this storefront is the largest scale logo I could think of.

I'm also a fan of prefabrication and it was important to me, in conjunction with the time limits that existed, to have the façade done in one piece, and delivered and installed quickly.

JS: The façade was fabricated in one piece off-site?

HK: It was fabricated by Western Artstone in Colma. It was brought in at six o'clock one evening and was in place at eight the same evening.

JS: And behind it is a sheet of glass?

HK: Yes, that is entirely independent of the façade.

JS: Whenever I look in the store, I wonder what was on your mind when you designed the trusses that span the ceiling.

HK: Well, on this store I just let myself go. I did not approach the store from the standpoint of creating a style that consists of one idea only. As you know, when you design something many things fall into place because of the limitations we run into, such as restrictions of structure, environment, lighting, and so forth. I knew this element, the trusses, had to serve as a mounting surface for theatrical lighting, and had also to serve as a mounting surface for the theatrical screens in the store.

JS: Are the screens still in place?

HK: Yes. The original idea was to change them every season rather than redecorate the store.

JS: Do they actually do that?

HK: No. Changing the screens has turned out to be a nightmare. Because the space is 18 feet tall, and because the screens have to be built structurally very soundly to be safe, it is not easy to move them. So, since they are in place permanently, we thought of hiring an artist to paint them every season. The problem with that is, the true artist really does not want to paint over somebody else's work, knowing he is going to be painted over by somebody else in three months. So, the screens now have a very neutral background and the change that occurs in the store takes place in the windows and other parts of the store.

JS: In the back of the store you have broken columns arrayed to suggest an infinity beyond the screens. Is the suggestion of infinity at that point something you consciously decided to do?

HK: Definitely. In my public spaces I always try to extend the vision beyond what you can see, not only to make the spaces appear larger but to give the observer a comfortable feeling of knowing where they are and that there is a way out.

JS: When I go into the store and see the handrails just inside the entryway I always laugh. Are they something you quickly sketched out?

HK: As architects, we arrive at a point where we find ourselves knowing too much. I've done quite a number of stairs and I always get to the point where I say to myself, Without repeating myself, how can I do this stair railing uniquely? It isn't for the sake of uniqueness that you do it, but because you don't want to repeat yourself. You have to be able to forget all the knowledge you have of the past, all of the intricate connection details, the code, and so forth, and just put a new handrail in place.

JS: You did the design for perhaps the most visible renovation of any building in San Francisco, the former Hamms Brewery, which was converted into a food services building. I drive by it every day going to the office, and I greatly admire the detailing of the new skin on the building. What is the exterior material?

HK: Pleco. It's an integral color finish for coating foam panels that supply the required insulation for the building. The color is pre-mixed, and you've only got one chance. You have to make a judgment in terms of the building's final overall appearance based on a two-square-foot sample on the wall, while the building is still under construction.

JS: What complications did you set for yourself here?

HK: There were more than enough to begin with. On the ground level, my desire was to introduce clarity to the plan of the space, for orientation's sake. So that when you enter the door you're automatically led to the elevator lobby, where you have two or three options. It's easy to understand where to go. I tried to bring in as much order as I could. The best way to do that was to create dynamic elements, such as the balcony form that looks like a Cuisinart's rotating device.

JS: When you talk about the job you don't seem nearly as excited as when you talk about the Jessica McClintock projects.

HK: I had absolute freedom on those other projects.

JS: But at the Hamms Building you greatly enhance a local landmark.

HK: I can't be the judge.

Above: Food Service Trade Center, San Francisco.

Left: Perspective section, Jessica McClintock Store, San Francisco.

Below, left and right: Food Service Trade Center, San Francisco.

Kotas/Pantaleoni Architects

Jeremy Kotas

 Jeremy Kotas and Anthony Pantaleoni began working together in 1981. Their special interest, as they describe it, is hard-core vernacular buildings. Jeremy Kotas has a diverse track record, including working for the Los Angeles architect Frank Gehry and with the San Francisco Planning Department. He reshaped his own neighborhood, Laidley Street in San Francisco, by designing a dozen buildings for it in as many years. Tony Pantaleoni studied briefly at the École des Beaux Arts and subsequently worked at Studio d'Architettura in Florence, Italy. He has taught at the City College of San Francisco and has won recognition for public and social service activities and fundraising.

JS: You admire the early Bay Area architect Ernest Coxhead, don't you?

JK: Yes. I thought that as I got older I'd be interested in fewer things; but, I'm actually interested in more things, and Coxhead is one of those things.

JS: Coxhead did a number of fine homes and churches.

JK: When I first came to the Bay Area, the late John Beach showed me pictures of his work. He did a church, St. John's, that has an upside-down kind of ice cream cone effect on top that seems to be a cross between a Buck Rogers space ship and a rural church steeple. It's way too large for its neo-Byzantine base, and at first you don't realize how tiny the building is. It looks immense, like Hagia Sophia, which in part it's based on.

I've been interested in buildings since I can remember. In particular, how bizarre they often are. That church is bizarre. These odd and strange aspects are often thought of as negative and people might say, Oh, that's a bizarre building. I would usually be interested in it and would feel bad sometimes that people thought it was odd or strange. It took a process of years for me to understand what was appealing to me.

Part of Coxhead's strength is his own personal sense of scale and his manipulation of things I'm sure were given to him by his clients as requirements. They probably said, Well, we want Tudor and we want the garage on this side, but we don't care about the living room. He would meld that all together and create some very powerful stuff. Many of my projects, especially the ones I've done for myself, are my way of playing like that, often with very little money. My former home, Laidley Castle, was similarly done. You know how it is with the first building you do. It was as though I might never do another, so I had to put everything into it I could think of. Since there was little money but lots of time the details got elaborated greatly.

The building was originally planned to be built in 1976, the twin bicentennial year, and I wanted it to reflect that fact. It was a chance to summarize and compact a lot of California traditions that are at war with one another.

JS: What are they?

JK: There is the example of any Maybeck garden pavilion you might find in Berkeley, just sitting there for you to go into when it rains. At the same time there is also the closed posture buildings in the city have, especially from the street, where all buildings are mysterious to some degree. There were also specific things, such as the fact that San Francisco was once nicknamed the City of Flags. Some buildings in town, especially in older areas such as the Tenderloin, have two and sometimes three flag-poles. If you go to the Tenderloin, you will find a wealth of spikes in the air. I thought the flags should be designed to be seen against the sky, not according to some patriotic mumbo jumbo. I preferred a yellow flag on the house, but the current owners usually have a purple or orange one.

JS: So you built it and sold it?

JK: That's right. I did a lot of the work on it myself, because I had worked on other houses and I wanted to see how far down that line I could go. It's a house I think of very highly, one of the best things I've ever done. It was an unrepeatable experience, in that I will never be able to again sit down and work things out to that level of degree and that kind of participation. And, frankly, I don't want to.

JS: I like the garage door used as a wall.

JK: That door works very well. When I lived there, if I were home on Saturday, the door would be open all day long, and wandering neighborhood dogs and visitors would come in and out.

JS: The house has an eclecticism and a variety of visual images, both characteristics of other work you've done. You certainly have a lot going on visually in the multiunit housing project on California Street in San Francisco, and at first glance, almost a kind of stylistic anarchy, although the more one looks at it the more it makes sense. Why is the building so visually active?

JK: This may not sound right, but if I talk long enough and fast enough perhaps you will agree. Do you know the joke about Mozart's music from the movie *Amadeus*? Someone criticized his music for having too many notes. He said, "Which ones are too many? Show me."

There is a lot going on because our client wanted a building that would match the Victorians he owns next door to the site. We told him

Left: California Street Apartments, San Francisco.

we weren't going to do a fake Victorian, although we did use elements of them as points for departure. In San Francisco people are constantly challenged with the problem of building right next to much older buildings, often Victorians, which, however deplorable they may be as works of architecture, are highly revered.

Because we had upzoned the property and had numerous height controls and code difficulties, we could not build the rather largish box we first intended. But, then I remembered a project of Frank's in southern California that he did as a cheap spec grouping in which each unit kept its identity in the overall massing of the project, and decided it would be a good point of departure.

JS: I know that project. It appears to be three plywood cubes that have been squeezed together and distorted.

JK: Right. This approach also solved the requirements of a very obscure city planning code requirement, Section 140, which requires that every dwelling unit must have one room that looks out to the street or out to a rear yard of minimum dimensions. When you put five units in a row you have problems. Donald MacDonald could probably tell you more about that than I. I now really appreciate what he's struggling with. But the result was that by breaking up this building into lots of little pieces, which solved many of the problems facing us, we finally created visual competition for the rich, ornate stuff on the adjacent Victorian without doing a similar design and details. What we did is create a lot of contrast. We have peaked roofs, they have flat roofs; we have many colors, they're bland; we have all these broken forms, they are one block. Without bowing to mimicry you couldn't ask for a greater contrast.

JS: I don't understand the awning over the front door to the first unit. To me it looks awkward.

JK: It's one more overlay that is very important here in the way it was important to Ernest Coxhead's work. He produced buildings that instantly conferred the sense of some age and, indeed, some aging, as though a building had been altered over time. And that sense is in this building from the massing on down to the detailing. When you look at this project you can almost say something like, Well, there was a house built way in the back, and then maybe it got some kind of a Bay Area style added on to it later, and then a piece was maybe tucked in over here near the front later on. The awning appears to have been added later.

JS: Your Erectheum house on San Francisco's Potrero Hill, with its porch of the mannequins, seems to be openly gay. There really is very little in San Francisco by way of architecture or public art that reflects the large gay population.

JK: This house reflected that fact, maybe more than it should have.

JS: The building has a plan that allows a couple to live separately while they are in the house, and has an absolutely wild vernacular on the outside. I mean, we have the Temple of Karnak

at the corner, and something akin to the Porch of the Caryatids on the side. At first glance it might be mistaken as a mausoleum for aerobics instructors.

JK: Actually, inside the column at each landing level is a phone booth. The scale play is again, like Coxhead. But a lot of this building was my first shot at decoration. You must remember, this was really before the word postmodernism was around much—I wasn't thinking that way. Now, I have to catch myself because it's all sort of, you know, the latest thing, or it was, anyway.

JS: You were ahead of your time?

JK: Well, maybe, in a sense. What I loved about this building was that it was the simplest kind of San Francisco vernacular building. And it was decorated to within an inch of its teeth. That phrase contains a lot of the intent in this house. But, best of all, it let me have the kind of twist I like best. I mean, the Greeks would probably criticize me for this, but I think the Porch of the Maidens helps make the Erectheum a deliberately light gesture in comparison to the Parthenon. I'm sure I knew as a child that the Parthenon was considered the perfect building. When I first heard of the Erectheum I was fascinated with the fact that it was imperfect. And then, later on, I realized that if someone asked me to design a building next to the world's most perfect building, I'm not going to try to do the world's second most perfect building. Makes sense. Anyway, when this job came along I thought of the Porch of the Caryatids and the Erectheum and gay life in San Francisco, and it just fell together. I really didn't design it, it happened to me.

JS: I like the design. But I think the mannequins on the porch are not done as well, or rendered as well as the design. Perhaps if there were a strong figurative tradition today in sculpture that might be different.

JK: Well, the mannequins were the first question that the client pushed on us. To them they were real people, not mannequins. But, you know there are mannequins you can get that look like real people. Part of the fun of this is the constant change involved. These guys should have their clothes changed with the seasons, you know. Swimsuits are great for summer, well, maybe not in San Francisco, or perhaps top hats and tails. . . .

JS: How did your clients react to the design?

JK: They were horrified.

JS: In addition to Gehry, I know you also worked for MLTW/Turnbull here in San Francisco. I can see the influence in your design for the Ulloa townhouses in the Sunset District.

JK: I couldn't tell you how strongly I've been influenced by those guys. This project is at Fourteenth Avenue in the Sunset, among a row of merchant builder's homes. The vernacular is Spanish colonial, or Mediterranean revival, of the kind done by George Washington Smith.

Above: Ulloa Street Townhouse, San Francisco.

Right and bottom: California Street
Apartments, San Francisco.

JS: Smith is without a doubt one of America's most underrated architects.

JK: Yes, he is. These buildings represent an idea of mine I've always liked, which is to fragment the building into pieces, or literal remnants or fragments. It has the forceful awkwardness of forms often found in vernacular housing. When you approach the house from the terrace, there is a big lump that you have to confront and face.

JS: You certainly do. I know you've put it there to emphasize what you call the awkwardness of the so-called builder vernacular, but, to me it simply looks out-and-out clumsy. I couldn't do it.

JK: Well, I think a certain awkwardness highlights the design. Some great English literary light said that without a certain awkwardness there is no great beauty.

JS: Of course, and every perfect thing has to have something imperfect, and all that. Still, it looks awkward to me.

JK: Well, it is. It's done that way more than somewhat deliberately. There is a minor level of jokes going on which relates the building to its immediate context. Unlike the builder boxes with the stuff in front, we have a real house shape, with the boxes in front. So there is that reversal. I mean, we're condemned by the rules of the Planning Department to be cement plaster like our neighbors, to have a big window and a bunch of little windows, and all sorts of stuff. But, they can't force us, at least not yet, into the same straightjacket of cuteness. I wanted to go as far away from the sweetness of those things as I could.

JS: You mean the Sunset row houses.

JK: That's right, the ones we're now condemned by the planners to look at as a standard of excellence. We know that they're no standard of excellence—they're just houses of a certain mediocrity. This house, hopefully, will not be like them. Yet it will coexist very happily with them because they share things in common.

JS: This kind of architecture seems to go somewhere without forgetting its past. Perhaps because of that it is San Francisco's late twentieth-century residential architecture.

JK: Well, it is.

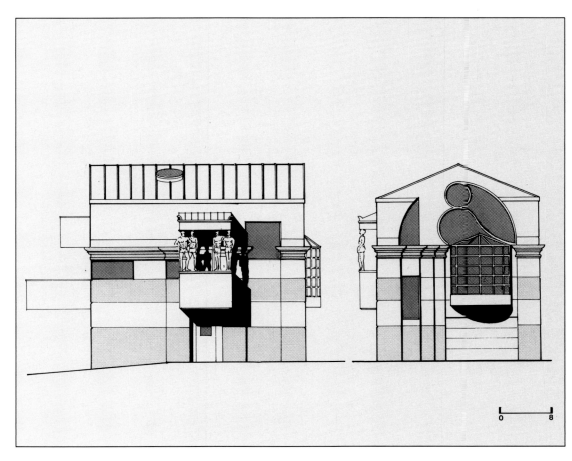

Right: Erectheum house, San Francisco.

Lars Lerup

Since 1970 Lars Lerup has taught at the University of California at Berkeley, where he is a professor of architecture. He has written and lectured widely. He also acted as Director of Educational Programs at the Institute for Architecture and Urban Studies in New York City during 1979–1980. His most recent book, *Planned Assaults*, is published by the Canadian Center for Architecture and the MIT Press. He also wrote *Building the Unfinished*, published in 1977.

JS: What is your role as an educator in architecture? What are you trying to communicate to your students?

LL: Allow me a bucolic metaphor: Teachers and students all work in the vineyard of architecture. Architecture is a subculture that has a long history. Even if some of its fundamental characteristics have died, I think success in architecture comes from maintaining and working in its vineyard.

JS: You think what has died?

LL: A certain kind of architecture has died. For example, when Le Corbusier designed Villa Savoye he pulled the original house out of the ground, took off the roof, and replaced it with a terrace. He argued that somehow architecture met the future and was on the way to resolving the problems of the city. His ultimate solution, the Algiers Plan, which has one singular building that solves all the problems of the city, does not work, as we now know. The hope embodied in the Algiers Plan, that architecture could be a social prophylactic, no longer exists. That kind of thinking in architecture is dead. Now, we have to find another role for architecture, which it turns out is not easy to do. You can adorn the "private" lives of the rich or great corporations, but that doesn't answer the hopes for architecture as a public good. Architecture once had relevance to entire societies. It was one of the many manifestations of human interaction, of human grandeur and folly. Now it has become the reflection of largely private concerns. I presume one can say that the kind of gaudy, 20,000-square-foot houses my colleagues are doing for rich people are somehow both follies and reflections of a society, but I don't think that's where architecture is. In some sense architecture for me is still public art that has and should have a public commitment.

JS: And a big responsibility to the public.

LL: Yes. Unfortunately, when this kind of doubt presents itself—that architecture doesn't solve social problems

Above: Goldstine Residence, San Francisco.

Below: Goldstine Residence, San Francisco.

and perhaps even makes them worse—we are somehow lost and don't really know what to do. Since I don't have an answer I investigate architecture's old structure and its own internal workings. And in the meantime I hope that something will come around and make architecture valuable.

I think there is an inherent ideological hope that every time you do something it's going to be better than what you did before. It's a utopia that's built into architectural practice that makes us always think of improvement. Or, that if you do as well as you can, and if you are lucky, you will do just as well as they did in the last classical building down the road. And that is not the kind of black hat and swinging cape attitude of many modernist architects.

JS: Frank Lloyd Wright.

LL: Yes, there is another kind of architect. I think we can learn something from that. Philip Johnson's argument that we are really all whores is something that I, for one, don't want to accept.

JS: It's repulsive when you think about it.

LL: The metaphor certainly is. It's antithetical to the history of the profession. There is a real decline when something like that takes hold. I mean, if you stop saying No to what you think are your client's incorrect desires you've lost it. You have to stand up for architecture.

JS: In your teaching and in your books, there is a sophistication in your approach to architecture seldom found in the workplace. Is it through your books and your teachings that you hope to influence architecture?

LL: It's hard to know how much my work is a desire to influence, or just the expression of what I'm able to do for the discipline. Despite all my reservations, I would still like to build. Anyhow, in terms of my written and speculative work, they are attempts to break through the everyday life of the profession to ask the fundamental questions about why we build and what we should ideally build. Perhaps even more important, they are attempts to question all the things we take for granted.

JS: Another way of saying that is that you have the luxury of being able to think about it. Unfortunately, the day-to-day practice of architecture is filled with running a business, detailing designs so that they don't leak, and things like that. You have a great responsibility.

LL: Yes, you have the responsibility to explore things that normally you don't have the time to explore. That's what I've done. I feel that the research part of the professional academician is very important. I'm getting some recognition for that now. It's been very rewarding for me because it turns out there are lots of people in

Above: Goldstine Residence, San Francisco.

practice who are very stimulated by my ideas concerning the discipline of architecture.

JS: You've taught for twenty years, including two at Peter Eisenman's Institute for Architecture and Urban Studies. You invited Eisenman to write the afterword in your most recent book, *Planned Assaults*. I want to ask you about his idea that goes something like "the essence of the act of architecture is the dislocation of an ever-reconstituting metaphysic of architecture." What do you think of that?

LL: That's the standard phrase of deconstruction. Jacques Derrida is the father of deconstructivism and sees as his task the undermining of all metaphysical positions. In other words, people like Hegel who seem so scientific and absolutely clear within their enterprise in fact have based everything on metaphysical presuppositions. Everything is ideology, particularly when it comes to architecture. Consequently, what Eisenman is arguing very strongly for is to make an architecture of our time. So, if our time is disjointed, so must be its architecture.

JS: Do you believe that?

LL: No. I don't buy into all of that because I think it is partially self-serving. I don't think we are in a particularly worse place than we have ever been in. Even if our world is more disjointed and incomprehensible than ever before, Eisenman's position is not the only reasonable response. In fact, I would argue that classical architecture may be more relevant than ever, since it attempts to achieve perfection in an imperfect world. I don't want to do it, but I think there is a form of classicism that might be absolutely appropriate for the dream of a perfect world. Anyway, since neither position can be the truth, it allows us all to make our own interpretation. All are reflections of our time.

JS: I believe the idea that architecture can provide harmony and comfort in the middle of chaos.

LL: I think that's perfectly viable. I'm somewhere in between. It's making a "fixed smile" that I'm skeptical about.

JS: A "fixed smile"?

LL: You know, the fake opulence so prevalent in postmodernist architecture. "Architecture-as-if."

JS: Trump Tower?

LL: Right. I believe in some kind of authenticity in terms of materials and construction. I like relatively transparent buildings in the sense that they can be read as things constructed and built.

JS: You say in *Planned Assaults* that "the NoFamily House is filled with expectations that are persistently frustrated." Why do you design a building that persistently frustrates its users?

LL: You have to think of these houses as being primarily didactic. It is for the reader to actually live in the NoFamily House. There is no intent of building it. By occupying the house on paper, the reader reflects on his own home.

JS: I wondered if the frustrations are thought of by you in the same way as Eisenman thinks of the famous column in the middle of the dining space in House VI.

LL: No. It is my notion that people would have to move into this house and repair it to make it usable. In that act of repairing is where the technology of the family would really be visible. In other words, where they have patched up the house is where you would see the reflection of the family.

JS: It solves the problem of someone who buys the speculative house that in no way reflects his own life.

LL: Exactly. In some ways this house is like Pessac, by Le Corbusier. The people who occupied the units put up pitched roofs. In some ways that's the sort of thing I was interested in doing. Because that is where the user really acquires the house, because they let their values butt up against the architect's values.

JS: Lars, in your book and in speaking with you here I get the impression that your ideas have a strong basis in politics.

LL: Yes, absolutely.

JS: Where would you say you stand?

LL: My ideas do have real problems with the present state, having grown up in Sweden and felt the overpowering vision of the state promoting a particular point of view. What I am more interested in is a kind of Jewish *stetl*: a community, or ghetto, where nobody's too big. No one completely overpowers anyone else. There is a kind of entrepreneurial spirit. I liked Apple Computer when they were very small. I like ambition for excellence.

JS: Do you think there is a Marxist influence in your book?

LL: Well, I guess I have been touched by Marxism. I'm not a Marxist in the political sense of the word, because I don't believe in the dictum that the proletariat is going to solve our problems. I don't believe in the totalitarian state.

JS: The reason I ask is that in *Planned Assaults* you said, "the conventional plan is a blueprint for the business of the family, the economics of love and fear." That sounds Marxist.

LL: You're pointing out something clearly inspired by Marxism, but that statement came from Michel Foucault and Kenneth Boulding. The notion here is that the house is a kind of disciplinary mechanism promoting a certain kind of economic behavior.

JS: But, it's not an attack on the middle class?

LL: No. It's hard to attack the middle class when you sit straight in the middle of it and enjoy it. I presume that in some sense the armature of the Marxist dilemma is there, though.

JS: In the foreword to your book, Phyllis Lambert says, "The NoFamily house challenges the function and the accepted social and economic

Top and bottom left: Goldstine Residence, San Francisco.

structures which engender the single family house across North America." What exactly are you challenging?

LL: In some way it's relatively simple. In school I ask my students to design a house, and I say do it right now. It takes about five minutes for them to come up with a plan that has a kitchen, a living room, two bedrooms, and a bathroom. Why is that? Why is it so kneejerk? Why do we have no other concept? Someone says that's the way we want to live. So much of the housing stock in this country has been in some sense speculative.

JS: Almost all of it is speculative.

LL: So we really don't know what we want anymore. It is something that has somehow been given to us by some complicated structure we take for granted. We should never take anything for granted. You shouldn't take love for granted, you shouldn't take social relations for granted, and you should always work on the world, if only to understand it better.

James Monday

 James Monday's interest in architecture began in the 70s when he worked as a printer with David Goines in Berkeley. Among the projects he worked on were books on architecture, which inspired him to obtain his architectural degree from the University of California, Berkeley. His office in Berkeley is in a space shared by a number of talented young architects, including Gary Parsons, Mark Toma, Karen Burks, Michael Shakespeare, Pam Burns, and Canan Tolon.

JS: You did the Goldstine House on Russian Hill as a joint venture with Lars Lerup. What attitudes of yours about architecture are embodied in the new house?

JM: The Goldstine House was built on the site of Imogen Cunningham's original home, which we tore down to construct the new buildings. We felt a certain attachment to the history of the original house, which was an earthquake shack built in 1906, because as a child, the client had a close relationship with Imogen and was very attached to the history of the original house. So it was important to us to indicate the volume of Imogen's house in the massing of the new house. Also, in a number of our earlier studies we tried to maintain the same slope and pitch of the first house's roof but were thwarted by the height restrictions of the city planning code. In order to somehow reflect the original roof we pitched the smaller roof, the seemingly clipped-on portion of the design, to match Imogen's roof, as a kind of memory device.

JS: I like the severity of the elevations very much.

JM: We were making references to the maritime quality of the district. We looked at a lot of buildings in the Marina district, to which we felt a distinct tie.

JS: But you were still incorporating references to the original earthquake shack.

JM: Yes. For instance, the green paint on the clipped-on portion of the design refers to the green paint used on the shacks. There must have been an abundance of green paint right after the earthquake.

JS: In the November 1988 issue of *Abitare*, Lars Lerup, speaking for the two of you, writes "when we were asked to design a house precisely in (a prototypical block of Russian Hill), it became clear that the fabric of the city was so palpable and dominating it had to rule our actions and we must remain its servants." Why must you be slaves to context?

JM: In this case we were dealing with a pretty strict set of rules about residential building, which were very tight constraints with regard to the zoning envelope. Those rules become very, very prescriptive in one sense, while being almost impossible to define because we were dealing with the bureaucracy of City Hall. We found ourselves facing completely ironic situations in which we would be in compliance with one set of rules as interpreted by one planner and in direct violation of another set of rules according to someone else in city planning.

JS: Can you give an example?

JM: Off-street parking. In order to provide one off-street parking space for this house the city loses two street spaces, because of the curb-cut into the garage.

JS: Part of the difficulty must have been that you needed variances for so much of the work and because the scope of the project kept changing.

JM: Yes. The initial variance we applied for was based on our first scheme, which was for a simple bathroom and bedroom addition. The next scheme, which was much larger but within the same footprint, was a partial second-floor addition, for which we received another variance. And then the scope increased again, which required applying for another variance. Finally, the project was reevaluated by the city as new construction, rather than as a remodel. In part our difficulties came from the changes in scope of the project, and in part from trying to create a building while the planning code was in a great state of flux.

JS: I think the code requirements will continue to change quite a bit over the next few years, as they continue to reflect the politics of San Francisco.

JM: Yes, they will. That is a great part of the struggle of building in San Francisco in our time.

Right and bottom: Goldstine Residence,
San Francisco.

Levy Design Partners

Toby Levy

 From her own renovated building on San Francisco's South Park, Toby Levy maintains an active practice involved in renovations, interiors, and new buildings. She is also active in the community, serving on the boards of many organizations, including the American Institute of Architects. She has taught at Columbia University, the University of California, Berkeley, and the California College of Arts and Crafts architecture department in San Francisco.

JS: How extensively did you renovate the two-story building that now contains your offices?

TL: The building was burnt out, with a bunch of punks living in it. We gutted it, seismically upgraded it, changed all the electrical and plumbing, took out almost all the walls, inserted a courtyard, and built a garage. Nothing is left of the original except the newel post at the top of the stairs.

JS: I know you went to some trouble to relate the building to the park. Just what did you do?

TL: South Park was originally designed to be like Bath, in England, or any of those places where there was a continuous façade along the edge of the park. When we bought the building it was flat-bayed, which was wrong because of its location at a very precipitous and important corner of the park. My first desire was to complete the curve of the park, which I did by giving the building a mastectomy—taking off one of its bays and filling out a new bay that completes the line of the park. When we completed the tangent to the park, that set up an angle that then could reverberate through the building by means of the geometry we used in designing the interiors.

JS: And the colonnade, which is quite strongly articulated inside, reflects that?

TL: It's on the line of the original bearing wall. Where it doubles up in the back is the area where the original column line shifted from defining a corridor to defining the kitchen and dining area. That's why there is a dual column line.

Another problem we dealt with is that the building is 20 feet wide at its broadest point, and 11 feet at its narrowest, but when you're in the office now you never feel that you're in a 20 foot by 92 foot building. That is in great part due to the angled geometry. Also important to me was the breaking out of the seismic cross-bracing wherever it occurred, and more subtle things such as references to the old type of paired window system that would have existed if this building had a more normal façade on its exposed property line wall.

JS: You thought it important to bring that out?

TL: Yes. On this project the contextual issues were dealt with in almost a packaging kind of way.

JS: So a great part of the design revolved around your interest in being contextual?

TL: Right, not only on the exterior, but the inside as well. That was very important.

JS: Why did you want to be contextual?

TL: Why did I want to be contextual? Because I think contextualism grounds architecture, physically and historically. It acknowledges the history of an area, both the present and the past. I think what we're going through in this present era, with all this faux marble this and patina that is people looking for a sense of grounding. Unfortunately, it's on a very superficial level.

JS: With your strong interest in context, I would like to know your thoughts on working in the Rincon Center development going into, on top of, and next to the very beautiful former post office on Mission near the Embarcadero. I haven't been inside but I think the exterior has been greatly damaged by the addition of the connecting walls between the stair towers on the roof. To me it's as if the renovation architects never really looked at what they had to start with, which is unfortunate, because the original building is such a fine addition to the city. How does one begin working in there?

TL: You should go inside. It's an excellent example of nouveau-deco. There are too many materials. The renovation architect reinterpreted deco so that it means, among other things, that there are nine or ten types of marble, four types of granite, five kinds of wood, two different types of storefront windows, and six types of everything else. It's incredibly overdone.

JS: Looking at the design of the shop you're doing in there, there seems to be a great deal of playfulness to it.

TL: I believe there is a lot of playfulness in the work of many good modernist architects, such as Richard Meier. I think his attitude leaves a lot of leeway for exploration. The problem with modernism is that it's come down to us as being primarily about functional diagrams, which is fine for office buildings, sort of. . . .

JS: It's not fine, even then.

TL: I mean, more for the building envelope. But, it's not fine for interiors. You can't decorate the world with beautifully detailed marble.

I explain to my clients that solving their functional needs is one thing, but giving them real architecture, which is what they really should have, is a gift. I mean, they are going to pay you just the same to do either one. But the real gift is the space they ultimately walk into, and it's something they never imagined.

Lyndon/Buchanan Associates

Donlyn Lyndon

 The principals of Lyndon/Buchanan Associates are Donlyn Lyndon and Marvin Buchanan. Donlyn Lyndon is a professor of architecture at the University of California, Berkeley, and is formerly head of the architecture departments at M.I.T. and the University of Oregon. He has twice been appointed Architect in Residence at the American Academy in Rome. Marvin Buchanan is a visiting lecturer at the University of California, Berkeley, and has been a fellow at the American Academy in Rome.

JS: What is the history of the science center you did for the Athenian School in Danville?

DL: The science center was preceded by a master plan we prepared for the school. During the planning we found out that originally the campus had been planned as four campuses surrounding a common library. That all fell apart, leaving the library cut off from the rest of the school. The first step we felt should be made with a new building was to increase the linkage to the library.

JS: How?

DL: We made the path to the library into something that confronts the science center, that becomes part of it. We also noticed in doing the planning that although there is an absolutely glorious climate there and the place is very wonderful, there were no well-designed outdoor spaces. We wanted to make nice outdoor places. There is an emphasis in our work on porches as gathering places. In the science center, a huge porch on the south side is a gathering spot connected to the vital parts of the building, including the science preparation area, the tiny little reading room, study carrels, and the faculty offices.

JS: And the roof forms reach up to the north light and become a visual transition to the hills?

DL: Yes. The two starting points for us were reaching for light in a correct way and providing a social edge to the building. There is a third consideration, also, which was fitting the building onto the edge of the hill. In other words, it runs along the edge of the contours and has a bend in it because it follows the contours. That made it easier to build, but also means that as your eye moves along the roofs their orientation shifts slightly, with a bit of the fluctuation that the hills beyond have.

JS: With regard to the site, how does the landscaping plan relate to your master plan?

DL: We had a number of discussions with the students, faculty, and staff about what they thought was important. As a part of the discussions, a landscape plan that could be done incrementally was worked out. It is related to the notion of rooms and spaces that respond directly to the outside and the idea of enhancing movement on the campus, because the site is so beautiful and so much of the students' time is spent outdoors. This was the first building to illustrate how that could happen. That's because it was developed with the direct participation of the students, faculty, and staff.

JS: With regard to how you've spoken about the primary importance of the client, I want to ask you about your Phoenix Townhouses, in Sacramento. Since they were built on spec, how did you envision the users? Isn't there a great difficulty in architecture when such enormous amounts of housing are built on spec for people who have absolutely no input in the design?

DL: Our way of imagining what the clients would want was through introspection. Introspection of ourselves as potential inhabitants, though, not ourselves thinking in terms of nifty design gimmicks. I think that's an important difference. One of the things people have observed about my writing is that I tend to confuse the use of the term *we*; that sometimes I'm talking "we" as designers, and sometimes I'm talking "we" as users. That is deliberate. As designers I think we have to act both roles. You need to constantly imagine yourself inhabiting the place, as well as designing it.

JS: Sure, but, I'm asking what do you do about not really knowing anything about the user?

DL: The fundamental core is having some sense yourself of the various kinds of living possibilities and the ways of living and being in things that there are: then, using those to have a discussion with the people around you. You have to be very humble about it, but that is where you start.

In this case we had a lot of discussions with the developers, and some discussions with their partner and sales advisor. When some of the first buildings were up, there was some discussion with the people who were running the sales office. We're shy about talking in terms of sales experience, though, because I firmly believe that the set of things hanging around sales are not the set of things important to living in the place. The sales issues are not often genuine. If you use that input what you're doing is refining the salability of the product but not the livability.

JS: In his article in *Architecture* magazine, David Littlejohn seems to think that the houses were a bit out of sync with the Sacramento market. Is that so?

DL: I think the part having to do with being in some way out of sync had to do with the issue of livable space versus salable space. We were interested and concerned in designing these to

make houses that would have fine spaces in them and that would have images in them that were not remote. We designed them to be places people could bring their own ideas to. We were determined to do this in a way that had real consequence, not just images glued on. If there was a bay window it was in a good place. If there was a set of paired doors they were organized to the interior as well as the exterior.

JS: It wasn't going to be another Blackhawk, a collection of salable images. (Blackhawk is a residential community near Danville composed of very closely spaced large homes designed in a variety of popular styles, sometimes three to a house.)

DL: Yes, everything was legitimate, and not glued on, so in that sense some of it was out of sync with conventional imagery. Our client was terrific. He wanted a community of houses with a sense of being established and permanent that were not baiting fashion. He had been involved with other architects who leaned toward what was fashionable and marketable at the moment in terms of image. That's not what he was after.

JS: In an article you wrote, "On Being Part," you say that any project is part of something more, and that being part involves having distinction. You then call attention to the fact that the number of named parts of building form has decreased dramatically in the twentieth century. That's very provocative. What do you mean?

DL: Reflecting on that made me realize that there's a level of attentiveness in architecture that comes from naming the parts of buildings. I don't mean that we should be paying the same attention to exactly the same things the classicists did. But it is clear that not having generated names for characteristics or parts of buildings means that there isn't the kind of common attention to, or common understanding about what the roles are for those parts of buildings. To a certain extent that is even supported by the notion that you mustn't use names too much in perception because it lets you characterize things as individual entities rather than as relationships.

When things have a name they count. We would do well to pay more of the kind of attention that has been paid in the past to the pieces of architecture and not leave everything open to manipulation and fluctuation, which is often destructive. There remains, however, a tension between having the named part, which you care about, and not getting so absorbed in the piece that you forget the relationship.

JS: In the same article you talk about the importance of the façade mediating between the public and private realms. How do you feel about buildings that are very expressive of their technology and that are drastically different from the rest of the buildings surrounding them and that don't speak much of the same language? In your article you condemn the recent State Office Building in Chicago by Helmut Jahn for having no sense of mediating between public and private.

DL: I don't want to be in the position of saying that any of the emerging vocabularies or emerging relationships are invalid in themselves. I do think, though, that a lot of current work is generated out of stories about the architect's way of working, and what he can say about why he did what he did. It becomes a codified game of clever design moves with a lot of emphasis on iconoclasm. I'm very much in favor of iconoclasm when it's breaking boundaries in order to create something that has real value to the people who are going to be in and around it. Iconoclasm just for the purpose of showing how smart and nifty you are doesn't interest me. I think it ought to be resisted.

I think there are varying strategies about one's role in society, and one that is *au courant* now and with which I don't agree is that you keep undermining everything so that some supposed real good can come forward or, more cynically, to suggest that nothing matters.

JS: Along the lines of deconstructivism?

DL: Right. Or, you can build on what's positive and try to pull it up and give it enduring form. And that is where I try to nourish and expand positive responses rather than simply undermine clichéd responses, as a focus.

JS: And in design you put a major focus on the input of the user.

DL: The most fundamental premise we have always operated around—when we were together at MLTW and later—and which influences my thinking today a great deal, is that the observer makes a place, not the architect. What we do is set up the conditions clients make into their sense of home and their sense of place. It's the interaction of their minds with what we set out that creates genuine places. That means, for me, that you have to remain in contact with those people. Now, that doesn't mean giving them their first expectation of what they're going to get.

We would like architecture to be that we're providing things they didn't expect but can connect to, and they're making things out of them that we don't expect. That's what nurtures an engaged and alive citizenry within its environment. That's the fundamental proposition. Now, the autonomous people would say that all those connections are going to happen anyway;

we should just do our thing. There is some truth in that. There is architecture that accommodates and easily collects those kind of associations, and there is architecture that excludes them and makes them alien. We don't want to make things alien.

JS: As late modernism is often accused of, rightly or wrongly.

DL: Yes. The other thing I would relate my own development and position to is what I understand to be the core of modernism. I don't buy at all the notion that what modernism was about was creating objects. Do you know the work of my father? He was an architect of great importance in southern California.

JS: I know his work. Maynard Lyndon. A modern architect.

DL: He did an absolutely magnificent house for himself, which is very little published, that's just a simple concrete frame with glass walls. Inevitably, my thinking is rooted there.

JS: How?

DL: The way I understand modernism through that house is that it was in great part about providing a house that was about the particular place it's in, about the kinds of views and living that can happen there. It was about putting a sort of tent down in the landscape from which you could experience and understand and cultivate the landscape. It was about setting up walls of glass in ways that allowed a clear experience of the view yet were responsible to the sun. It was not about showing how cleverly you put together steel and glass. It was about how you move through things, and about providing real benefit to people who are using it. That's the fundamental.

Left: Phoenix Townhouses,
Sacramento.

Below: Athenian School, Science
Center, Danville.

MacDonald Architects

Donald MacDonald

 Donald MacDonald's work ranges in scale from massive land plans to do-it-yourself furniture. A strong advocate of low-cost housing, he was one of three American architects invited to attend the 1987 World Peace Forum in the Soviet Union. Donald MacDonald graduated from Columbia University in 1963 and began his own practice in 1966 in San Francisco, after teaching at the University of California, Berkeley. In addition to work for clients, he develops a number of his own projects.

Top left: City Sleeper.

Bottom left: low cost housing, San Francisco.

Top right: low cost housing, San Francisco.

JS: You've done some beautiful condominiums in the city for upper-income markets and received a fair amount of recognition for them. How did you get into low-cost housing?

DM: I did it because Mayor Feinstein said we couldn't do affordable housing in the city. I said, That's nonsense. And I did it free of all government money. I undersold redevelopment by $20,000 to $40,000.

JS: The plans for the low-cost houses are very clever in the way they divide up space into multiuse areas. I read somewhere that you believe we're all conditioned to a mythology of space we don't really need.

DM: Yeah. In America we don't understand that some people can live a whole life in a van and be very happy people. It's their van and they can lock it up, leaving their things in it while they work someplace else.

I can build a small but comfortable house for $12,000. You know what the mortgage is on that? About $120 a month. I've got one now that is 14 by 17 feet. They're a little odd, but if the government gives them the land they can sell the thing for $15,000. Right now, the government subsidizes one-bedroom apartments for $550 a month. That would support a house that cost $55,000 to build. It's bizarre. You know, the problem with building low-cost housing is that the regulations keep getting tougher and tougher, more middle-class.

JS: You mean code and energy requirements?

DM: Yeah. They knock up the price of a house $30,000, and wipe out hundreds of thousands of people because they add $300 a month to the mortgage. We need a two-tiered system of requirements at different income and cost levels. It's complicated, but it's more humane, because it reflects your needs.

JS: Parts of the code don't make much sense. For example, stair requirements and ceiling height minimums.

DM: If you compare the cost of a stair from one floor to another within a unit built conventionally to a safe ship's ladder, you're talking thousands of dollars to a few hundred dollars. The steeper

the ladder the less it costs. You say, come on guys, not everybody is eighty years old. There are ways around it, but you have to be prepared for lawsuits. I'm chipping away at it. We'll see how it goes.

JS: I read the speech you gave in Michigan when you won that state's competition to see who could provide the best low-cost housing. You said, "The excluded and disenfranchised have no investment in political stability. People who live comfortably in suburbia should give serious thought to the consequences of confining large numbers of people to economic ghettoes." I live near the Haight and it's true that many of the people there don't really care about economic or political stability as long as they can get a roof over their heads.

DM: You get a lot of abuses to property and the system when there's no chance or fair play for many people. There's no reason, absolutely no reason in our system, that every person can't have their own private space.

JS: How do we go about getting that kind of attitude into our American way of life?

DM: It starts with the homeless. My firm built 4 × 4 × 8 foot plywood enclosures, City Sleepers we called them, and put them under the freeway in the parking lot next to the office.

JS: Who lived in them?

DM: I started off with two alcoholics. One of them, George, lived in one of them for about eight months. When they moved in the first thing they did was stop drinking, which I couldn't believe. That lasted for three months. They'd come home from work and go to sleep. Pretty soon they started drinking again and in three months George was a goner. He died of acute alcohol poisoning. He was forty-two years old and just a nice human being who couldn't control what he was doing. He said that I was the first man in seventeen years who treated him like a man. After that, a woman who was a heroin addict and her child moved in.

The idea is that as a nation, as a group of human beings, we shouldn't dispel people as garbage. Even if they are different from us, if they want to live outside all the time, we shouldn't be harsh on them, because they have enough problems of their own.

JS: Why are the City Sleepers gone now?

DM: The parking lot I lease is under the freeway, so it's under CalTrans' jurisdiction. Four months after I put the units in place I began to get threatening notices from CalTrans. They finally sued, so I fought it for about eight months until it settled when it hit the California Supreme Court. I was just delaying, to implement the program on a bigger scale. But, it was finally settled that I would remove them. That was very traumatic for me because I had to throw this woman and her child into the street with all their possessions. It was awful. Here I am trying to move them off the lot, and the kid's crying, and I mean, it was terrible. I lined her up with a place, but she probably won't go into it.

JS: We've got hundreds and hundreds of acres under freeways. Couldn't the government provide that land for housing?

DM: The people in the neighborhoods won't let them. A guy who's got a $200,000 house doesn't want a one-room house next to his. That means that the state's got to come in and subsidize a two-bed and one-bath unit. We have a crazy perception of spaces, an upper-middle-class idea of what space means.

JS: At 4 × 4 × 8 feet your units are obviously minimum space.

DM: That's right. What you really learn as an architect from this is how important privacy and your own lockable space is. Usually in homeless shelters, the people in charge watch the homeless who sleep there. They do a body search before they let them in, and take away their dignity, the only thing they have. The homeless don't have anything. The authorities make sure of that. If someone goes down to the Salvation Army for a meal, he has to pray.

JS: It's the search-and-convert school of aiding the poor. What do you think of the contemporary scene in architecture in general?

DM: All the top-notch architects are fighting for a small, top piece of the profession. We're getting so esoteric, so avant garde, and so abstract, running around writing all these silly essays that have a thousand adjectives and adverbs to say some simple thing. All of our gods in architecture seem to be up in the air somewhere. This is while there are many, many homeless who need shelter. We're highly trained problem solvers. There is a real need for our talents in America.

Above top: Day Care Center, Stanford University, Palo Alto. Bottom: Low-cost urban housing.

Facing page top and bottom: low cost housing, San Francisco.

Mack Architects

Mark Mack

A native of Austria, Mark Mack has practiced as an architect in the Bay Area since 1978. In partnership with Andrew Batey until 1985 and now on his own, he has worked to develop a unique attitude toward architecture which he and Batey named neoprimitivism. A legacy of his in the Bay Area is the Western Addition, which he cofounded in 1976, and which was devoted to discussions and lectures on fine architecture. This organization has since become the Western Edge and functions under the auspices of the San Francisco Museum of Modern Art. He also cofounded the periodical *Archetype*. In addition to being published widely in America, his work has found a very receptive audience abroad.

JS: One night in the 70s I was sitting in Mario's Bohemian Cigar Store in San Francisco next to the architect Steve Holl, who was drawing a building of yours in the Napa Valley on a napkin for an architectural critic. I believe the house was partially underground.

MM: That was our first house, the Goldman House, which we called the Antivilla. It was within a villa concept but was buried and made to recede. It was all the opposites of what a villa in open land stands for. It's not on any kind of axis, it has no frontage, and it's tucked into the hill.

JS: Is there in the Antivilla a broader comment about big, dominating villas on the landscape?

MM: No, it was just specific to that particular job, but it embodied other aspects of our work which became more conscious in the next steps we took. One was my interest in one aspect of American architecture, the small industrial building type made out of concrete block with steel sash windows. I found a great honesty in the way those things were constructed. I was coming from a modern tradition where that sort of construction and materiality has a sort of moralistic value or undertone. I also rejected the kind of pretension in American architecture that tried to hook onto some kind of historic verification. I was looking for something that is America's own that I could relate to a modern building, a building of its time. I was also very impressed with the precision the blocks were done with, because in Europe those blocks are just for infill and are beat up and not precise. All of the industrial windows followed a kind of module that was rational.

JS: In Sally Woodbridge's book on Bay Area houses, she describes the houses following the Antivilla as being developed more along rationalist

Above: Gerhardt Residence, Sausalito.

Left and below: Gerhardt Residence, Sausalito.

lines of a neoprimitive philosophy. How does this broad use of "rational" fit your work?

MM: Rational had become at that time a word associated with a certain style advocated by people such as Aldo Rossi, Mario Botta, Leon Krier, Massimo Scolari, and others. There was a whole sort of movement about rational architecture that was about not only the rationality of your decisions but was also indicative of your style. It was a certain attitude that had to do with typology, that is, taking elements in a city fabric, or in a house fabric, and abstracting them while keeping them intact and making different compositions. For example, a window was a window, not an idiosyncratic expression. A door was a door, a house was a house, and up from there.

JS: So there was an abstracting of forms or a boiling down to their most literal forms. Some designers value the idiosyncratic or the personal. Is there a rejection of that in the rationalist work?

MM: Yes, I think it's somehow diverted. Rationalism doesn't deny that there is idiosyncracy and personality. But it occurs within a larger framework.

Another idea in the Antivilla is that of generic rooms. We did not call out individual rooms such as living room or anteroom. It read as five different rooms of varying sizes. That came, again, from my European background. In Europe houses are there for much longer than an individual's personal taste. In Austria things get passed on from family to family. There's a lot of remodeling, whereas here people just move to another house or find another neighborhood. Real estate is a whole different concept here. In that sense the house was a criticism, or a different value to be stressed. Also, within the generic room concept was the idea that you could take away the ornament, in the Adolph Loos sense, and use that money on making the room a little bit bigger. All of that fit into the primitivism of the work. We used the term primitivism because at that time, the era of postmodernism, everything had to have a name or you wouldn't be heard. We took it all in a sort of tongue-in-cheek way. Primitivism has both moral and sensual undertones. In art, however, it means something different. It's Picasso and his African masks, or cave paintings, or the romantic aspect of the islands. Another aspect is the romantic primitivism of the enlightenment.

JS: Although you say they aren't connected, there was a rise of primitivism in art at the same time, such as in the work of A. R. Penck and other artists. Do you think your work shared a common turning away from the slick or mass-produced concepts and images that had lost their power to something with a more gut-level power to it?

MM: Yes, that was one aspect of it: looking for an emotional connection to what you do, a connection to a more fundamental way of doing architecture, which is going back to Laugier's idea of the primitive hut, a constant purification process.

JS: You see Laugier as more of an inspiration than a justification?

MM: Right, exactly.

JS: Because I've heard architects working in the modern mode say that they see your use of the primitive hut as a way of justifying your work. Some of them have built their own technologically advanced huts as a way of saying that the primitive hut is not only a justification for primitivism but a way to justify buildings that are very expressive of their technology. You're saying it's more of an inspiration.

MM: Yes. It's not a literal inspiration even though in some aspect we might have taken that route. It's much more a stripping back to essentials. We used Laugier as a kind of cleansing agent. I felt at that time it was very important to get rid of some of the tensions and attitudes of postmodernism. We wanted to find our own definition. Neither Andrew nor myself are architectural intellectuals, like Eisenman, who would take the position that what we need now is a totally new reading of architecture because we are in a different time and are totally disconnected to anything that went before. Eisenman would put everything through something like an Aristotelian grid justified by something like mathematics and apply the site-specificness to that. I have never had much affinity for that—it's not material enough. For me building is still dimension and construction and building. For verification I looked at people like Louis Kahn, Luís Barragan, Hans Hollein, Aldo Rossi, and Mario Botta, who were doing things in an architectural tradition. They were not paper projects.

JS: Is your work a rejection not only of the applied styles of postmodernism, but also technology in general? I read once that you and Andrew were against highrises.

MM: To a certain degree. I have never found any justification for the way those things are done except for corporate pride and land speculation. There are ways to achieve density, intricateness, and urban scale by not going more than four stories. Vienna, Milan, Barcelona, and Paris are examples of this.

JS: I read a recent article about Richard Rodgers, one of the architects of Pompidou Center, in which he says that in the twentieth century with the capabilities we have, the best way to build, and the most beautiful way to build, is by expressing the technological capabilities we have. You must have an argument with that.

MM: Yes, Andrew worked with Norman Foster, another technology expressionist, in England, and wasn't totally enamored with their philosophy. To me, it is another way of doing a style, or cladding, which is not totally resolved and totally honest. To achieve the flexibility they talk about you have to spend much more money, and the need for flexibility is never as great as they imagine.

JS: A lot of those things get put in one position and are never moved.

Above: Gerhardt Residence, Sausalito.

Facing page top and bottom: Gerhardt Residence, Sausalito.

Above: Sunar furniture showroom, San Francisco.

Facing page top and bottom: Sunar furniture showroom, San Francisco.

MM: Yes. It's more of a style. If you look at the Shanghai Bank or Lloyd's of London, it's much more an expression than an idea that has anything to do with flexibility or something like that. Rayner Banham wrote an article on the Lloyd's building, saying that the bathrooms, because of their individual custom attachments and extravagant level of detailing, are more pretentious than bathrooms in a palace, because they are so precise and were done so deliberately by the draftsmen working on the project. Therefore, the argument that they are using technology in a nonornamental way doesn't make sense. Also, the level of building technology hasn't really advanced if you look at early twentieth-century examples or at cast-iron buildings.

JS: One of your criticisms of the work is that it is more style conscious than the practitioners admit. Hasn't the work of rationalist architects become a style? I read an article recently in which Kenneth Baker, art critic for the *San Francisco Chronicle*, said that it's impossible to do an abstract painting today because abstraction is just another genre of painting, and anything painted in the abstract immediately reads "abstract painting." Don't you have the same problem?

MM: I think you always face this problem. There is no way out of it unless you don't stand still or if you lose your important connections. I'm very close to the connections. I make almost literal connections to Barragan. But, I think it's what you pick that has to be charged. For example, when I look at Barragan I'm not seeing so much a particular intersection of two walls as I am a particular kind of break or symbiosis of modern form with a certain vernacular and a site-specific relationship. I mean, I'm not an inventor. There are so many things out there that can be brought into the spectrum. Our work has the element of trying to bring into the Bay Area a larger set of reference points. When we try to do a climate-related, site-related house we don't look at what's built on Russian Hill by Willis Polk, or in Berkeley by Maybeck. We look at Spain or Mexico, or regions that have similar climatic connections.

JS: Do you see yourself as a regionalist architect?

MM: Only in the sense that I am a reluctant regionalist, like Richard Fernau and Laura Hartman. I feel an affinity to people like Gardner Dailey and William Wurster, who had a reinterpreted attitude to regionalism, to site, and a reductive attitude.

JS: That reductivist kind of approach is quite apparent in the Sunar showroom you did in San Francisco's Jackson Square area.

MM: They wanted to have something very flexible, not too costly, but with a personal mark to it. I used the idea of the runway, or portico, to divide the space into private and open areas. I feel in most cases that separation between public and private is lacking in the American system of things. In Europe a house is much more a castle. It's much more privatized within

Above: Sunar furniture showroom, San Francisco.

the house, so that there are public and private rooms. In Vienna when I went to visit friends I generally never got beyond the powder room, or living room, or hall. In America it was so strange to me, especially on the West Coast, when I came here. I mean, you go to the home of people you don't know and they show you the whole house.

JS: I think often there is guilt associated with privacy here.

MM: Yes, and it's automatically associated with something nasty. Because there is not enough separation between the private and the public realm everything becomes public. For instance, a presidential nominee gets kicked out because he had an affair, which might be justified in his own terms, but it's not possible as a candidate. There is this pretense that this is good for the public, but because there is no real outlet it becomes thought of as nasty. Europe is very puritan, too. But, there are certain limits.

In architecture the lack of privacy creates real schisms between people. They're not allowed to have fences or walls over three feet high. And there is the three-foot side-yard setback between buildings, which creates real dead space. It creates a noise problem, which wouldn't be there with zero lot lines and things like that. So, in my houses I try to be very clear about what is public and what is private.

Robert Overstreet

 Robert Overstreet works out of his dramatic hillside home in Marin County's Corte Madera. Perched on a hillside near Mount Tamalpais, the house contains a fine sense of repose and containment in its interiors. Robert Overstreet is a native of Louisiana and has practiced in the Bay Area for many years. In addition to his mausoleum designs, he is the architect for Oyama Houseboat, perhaps the finest structure of its kind in the Sausalito houseboat harbor.

Above and right: Mausoleum, Italian Cemetery, Colma.

JS: You are most well known for the mausoleum projects you've done in San Francisco's necropolis, Colma. How many have you done?

RO: Well, the first one was in 1968. I guess I've done about a dozen since then. The Italian Cemetery is the most successful, and has done extremely well selling space in the new mausoleum buildings. When I began doing work for them, their business was going downhill. They had us master plan the site from scratch. They have sold very well since then.

JS: What is the derivation of the forms in the mausoleum in which you wrap the skylight down to the ground plane? Was it your desire to make the building as transparent as possible?

RO: It's very simple. Number one, the mausoleums of the past are quite dark and dim. They're depressing. Natural light is very important to counteract that. Number two, the colors are usually quite drab. I think color is important to make the space attractive, so that you don't think of death the same way you would in a dark and drab mausoleum.

JS: You don't want the space to be cryptlike in the traditional sense.

RO: Right. A crypt is really just a filing cabinet. It's the architect's role to organize them and provide an appropriate architecture. The odd thing is that the sales in these buildings are dependent on the view.

JS: On the view?

RO: A crypt that is close to the view is usually the most desirable. So the requirements of light, color, view, and some attractive landscaping suggested a continuous skylight returning to the ground providing both natural light and a view as well as landscaping. The buildings in Colma, as a whole, also try to integrate with the mound upon which they sit.

JS: I think these are fine buildings. Has this work led to other commissions of this kind?

RO: Strangely enough, no. As you probably can guess, people involved in cemeteries are very reserved and very traditional. They wouldn't believe that architecture like this leads to high sales. This is in contrast to the Italian people, who have a tradition of mausoleums and are not conservative with regard to design.

JS: Your work stands apart dramatically from much of the architecture currently being done in the Bay Area. It in part comes from a similar vein that Frank Lloyd Wright and Bruce Goff descend from, an architecture that claims to have its roots more firmly in America than in Europe. Where do you stand philosophically?

RO: I'm not very good at words, but let me give you just a little of my background. I first went to Tulane University, where the Navy V-12 program absorbed me during the Second World War, and I was transferred to the University of Texas. I had difficulties at that school. Of course, in those days it was verboten to have any influence by Wright, and I found his work very appealing. I returned to school in Texas after the war and did not get along well at all. I had heard that the University of Oklahoma was a good school, so I went up there one weekend and met Bruce Goff. He was very informal and very warm. His architecture just knocked me out. So, I went to Oklahoma and was very influenced by his work and I guess what you would call romanticism in architecture. My real beginnings were in a very rational and down-to-earth approach to architecture. My father was an architect. I was influenced by him at a very early age. I worked for him for a brief time after I graduated, but we sometimes didn't get along, and I thought it best for me to strike out alone. I worked in Seattle for about four years before coming to San Francisco. I started my own firm in 1963 with a partner, Elmer Botsai.

I believe that if you listen to your client and are familiar with the basics you need to know, and understand the program, that things often fall into place in terms of a general concept. I think a great deal of rationality occurs, even in the work of the so-called American romantic architects. Many people will look at Goff's work and not realize that he was a very rational designer. He looks wild, and so forth, but if you've ever seen any of his paintings you see how mild his architecture was compared to the imagination shown in many of his paintings.

When Goff presented a project to his clients he did so by showing them a series of overlays that began with a very schematic idea and evolved into a finished design. When they saw the final product they understood the reasoning behind it. He considered the aesthetic attitudes of the clients as well. He wouldn't have been able to sell these things to them unless he knew them pretty well, and knew what they could accept aesthetically.

JS: Have you worked with partners or on your own?

RO: I've had a number of partners over a period of time. I decided three years ago that my partners and I were just going in different directions and decided to separate from them. I was interested in the design aspect of things, and my partners were doing very well in remedial work on faulty buildings, and that was their thing. I didn't want to be known for doing remedial work on faulty buildings.

JS: Your plans are very clear and well-resolved. It seems that sometimes the plans developed by people affected strongly by Wright and Goff are extremely convoluted and fussy.

RO: I think some of them are designed from the outside. Inside and outside are not thought of as one.

Left: Mausoleum, Italian Cemetery, Colma.

Stanley Saitowitz Office

Stanley Saitowitz

 Stanley Saitowitz practices what he calls geological architecture. He received his bachelor's degree from the University of the Witwatersrand, in Johannesburg, South Africa in 1974, and his master's degree from the University of California, Berkeley. In addition to his buildings, he produces beautiful drawings that elegantly express his concerns in architecture. The Walker Art Center, in Minneapolis, is organizing an exhibit of his work to be shown in 1990.

JS: You said in your recent article in *The Architectural Review*, "Architecture involves reorganizing matter to form space. All material originates from the ground. Our activity of remaking the crust of the earth, our act to capture space on its horizon, can be viewed as geological." You go on to say "the instinctual play of housemaking, which we are schooled to forget, remains in all of us: like eating and breathing we all know the act of sheltermaking." You sound as though you believe creating one's own home is a genetic desire.

SS: It's literally true in the African culture I described in the article. In that much more integrated system there isn't a specialty of architecture. To some degree it's true in our society. It's just that the level is much more induced. It's like people choosing furniture, which is their way of housemaking. What that implies for architects, and what is a thread in my work, is the question, At what point do you leave things out to allow for the act of inhabiting?

Total design in the Miesian sense doesn't appeal to me. I'm interested in a much richer set of possibilities and the kind of architecture that allows a good degree of inhabiting. The idea of an imperfect architecture appeals to me, as opposed to the kind of classical view of the object which can have nothing added or subtracted. Of course I would like to design as much as possible of a house, and design the furniture as well, but, in some sense I understand the point of the occupant inhabiting the space. It's like the Eames House, which is filled up with the occupant's own creations and collections, versus the Parthenon, you know, which is thought of as being perfect within itself. It's that never-completed aesthetic that interests me.

JS: You also say in the same article that "dressed and decorated buildings—like clothing—speak of dreams and emotions, and express even the deepest selves of the people they house." Again, you're speaking of a tribal culture, but how do you regard embellishment and detail in your own work within our culture?

SS: I think the Kahn idea of ornament as opposed to decoration is what I'm interested in, the idea of the ornament being kind of an elaboration of the joint, so that the ornament is actually the act of constructing. The act of construction can be decorative, not in the sense of masquerade or make-up, but in the sense of amplification. It's the difference between putting on a mask and putting on make-up.

JS: I recently saw in the Metropolitan Museum some beautiful wall panels from Roman houses which were very simple and very beautiful. They were vertically proportioned, quite dark, and had a single line running up them through the middle with a small god or goddess at the top surrounded by a few leaves. It's decorative, but integral to their conception of what a building is. Is there room for that in your work?

SS: One of the things my work is about is a clarifying of certain intentions through the use of color, so that certain systems are described in color. I'm not a purist in that I'm against decoration, but in light of postmodernism or this very optical view of architecture we've been involved with in the last few years, I try to avoid the idea of just image as a way of understanding architecture. My concerns with architecture are spatial and experiential.

JS: When you spoke of the Bay Area in the same text it was in terms of geography and how the land forms here shape the buildings.

SS: What I wrote there is really an attempt to explain the approach in my work, which is involved very much with almost a phenomenological redescription of a given situation. I need to distinguish that from regionalism, because I think regionalism is a kind of stylistic impulse, and involved with image. If you think about the Bay regional style, it's a kind of blanket aesthetic for work that happened anywhere in the Bay Area. To my mind it's actually an uninteresting way of making architecture. I mean, if I go into Bill Stout's architectural bookstore I'm moved by almost any book I find there in terms of the weight of the information it carries about architecture throughout the world. I know there are architects in this area who set themselves up in the lineage of the original Bay Area architects, such as Bernard Maybeck or Ernest Coxhead. I think it is very limiting to model your architecture on that. However, I'm interested in the same kind of basis, which is that architecture is specific to where it is. Geological architecture is actually a kind of extension, in a very specific way, of its site. And it anchors us to where we are, as a way of knowing exactly where we're located. That's the power architecture has. It's of a particular place. I mean, a house at Stinson Beach, which is next to the ocean, is totally different from a house among a group of redwood trees.

JS: Each of the homes you've shown me looks quite individual.

Left: Goldberg Residence, Tiburon.

SS: In some ways that's a problem, because clients will come to me and not know what their building will look like when it's done. Looking at the work, it's difficult for them to say that I do this or that. They have a difficult time, which is true for me as well, because I don't start with a sense of what the end will be.

JS: The house you've designed for Stinson Beach north of San Francisco certainly looks and feels specific to its location.

SS: The house is about the meeting of the land and the water. The beginning of the house is the car, which is how these people arrive from the city. And the other side of the house is where they escape with their boat, so that the house is a bridge between the city and the ocean. It's about the resonance of the waves. The house creates a parascopic moment that magnifies where it is and acts as a focus to capture that particular place. I think that's very important for architecture to do that.

The fact is that today we live with many distorters of reality, such as television. I can turn it on and be more in tune with El Salvador or South Africa, or wherever, than here. I think architecture has always been a force to counteract that kind of artificial reality of illusion. That's why I'm interested in the realism of life with regard to where it is and how it anchors itself.

JS: So the sounds of the sea roll in over the beach and into the house at Stinson, and the building focuses that?

SS: Not exactly. When the clients first told me the site was at Stinson Beach I was quite excited, because I thought it was going to be a beach house. But, the site turned out to be on Seadrift, which is a lagoon, so what was left for me was not the visual character of the place, but the aural. Since the view is of other houses, the twisting in the house is about trying to dislocate your view, and give it more breadth. The other important thing was to make the sound of the waves come into the house. It's in a way like a shell or a cave or something with which you actually try to catch the sound of the water and bounce it into the building. Also, when you look at the section of this house it's almost as if it were carved out by the waves. When I did this I was thinking of that amazing sea wall at Ocean Beach, where you almost get the water turning. That's the sense the Stinson Beach house has.

JS: Let me ask you about another project. I think the model of the house you've designed for the Oakland Hills is quite beautiful. It sits nicely on the site. Many of the remaining building sites in the Bay Area are dramatically sloped.

SS: It is a very direct response to the site. The basic lines of the site almost establish the form of the house. In the design of the house there are two systems operating. One is the building envelope and the other is the relationship to the topography. It's a low-budget hillside house, so we are trying to minimize the moving of earth. The most logical thing to do is to follow the topography. The house is conceived as a

shape with a large roof that envelopes a very generous volume. The other interesting aspect to this house has to do with quite specific pragmatic issues. The house is for a very unique situation, a family that involves parents and a son with his wife, and someday perhaps children. So the building is really two houses that are joined by a communal kind of house.

JS: Does the interior column arrangement and general layout echo the plan of the pier and grade beam foundation?

SS: Yes. It's very logical. After the foundation the glu-lams are put up first, which means that you've established all your lines and can begin to frame. It's not that tricky, except for a curved wall, which always makes people jittery.

JS: I taught architectural design last summer with Ivan Kadey, one of your associates. He said that your career, your architecture, is what you basically live for, and that it's your reason for being.

SS: Pretty much. You know, when you have five houses to work on simultaneously you don't have time for much else. Because a house is an incredibly demanding thing, and I could do just one of them at a time. I mean, there's so much in just one of them, and every one of them is quite different. I have to keep each of them clear, which takes a tremendous effort. But, I love to bounce around, and it's very good. I'm happy to have work.

Above: Sukkah, Jewish Community Museum, San Francisco.

Facing page top and bottom: Quady Winery, Madera.

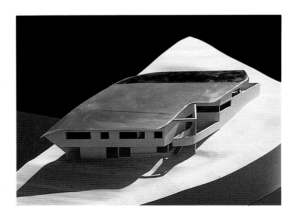

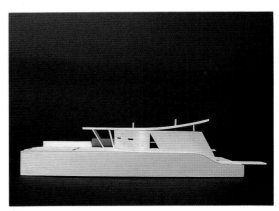

Top: Private residence, Oakland. Bottom: McDonald Residence, Stinson Beach.

James Shay

James Shay practices residential and commercial architecture from his warehouse-loft office in San Francisco's South-of-Market area. The following interview with the coauthor of this book was conducted by architect William Leddy (Tanner Leddy Maytum Stacy), who also read and commented on portions of *New Architecture San Francisco* while it was being written.

WL: Two of your most recently completed homes in San Francisco, your own and the Curtis residence, share a dynamic spatial interior organization typified by strong vertical volumes interpenetrated by horizontal elements. Spatially, your house has an almost theatrical quality to it. What do you think about architectural space in residential buildings?

JS: The house my wife and I live in on Edgewood was specifically designed to have spatial drama and to recognize art, by providing areas to display it and by containing my painting studio. At the time it was built I was single, so the house became very individualized. It really is an artist's loft turned vertically. The painting studio is on the lower floor. If we stay in the house we will have to remodel. Otherwise, young children could fall three stories to their doom.

WL: And the same is true in the Curtis House?

JS: No, not at all. That house is carefully segmented for acoustical privacy and is spatially fairly traditional. The multilevel volumes in it are only at the stairs. Part of the townhouse problem is to make going up and down stairs enjoyable, because we're doing it all the time. And, because of the narrow lot widths in San Francisco, houses can become claustrophobic. It's important to bring light, volume, and interesting circulation into the interiors. Stair areas are a natural place to do it.

Above top and bottom: Curtis Residence, San Francisco.

Left and below: Curtis Residence, San Francisco.

WL: You've had an experience that among architects is becoming increasingly unique in being able to design and build your own home. What lessons have you learned by doing it?

JS: Because the house is so open, I think a lot about how to provide spatial drama without compromising privacy. And I've learned a lot about the practical aspects of design, such as closet and kitchen layout, because I have to live with mine every day. Also, I know how it feels to pour a great deal of one's own money into never-to-be-seen concrete and steel piers drilled thirty feet into the ground.

WL: The façade of the Curtis house is significantly more complex in its use of color and form than your own house. Why?

JS: I wasn't satisfied with the façade on the first house. I never liked it compositionally. It's just not resolved. So, on the Curtis house I spent much more time on the façade. I wanted to do a complex façade.

WL: Why?

JS: I like a certain amount of complexity in things. I was also influenced by a building by Maki in downtown Tokyo that has a complex façade.

WL: The Wacoal Center.

JS: I love that elevation. Do you?

WL: Not as much as his other buildings. So what it really comes down to is a matter of aesthetic preference rather than a response to existing conditions or context?

JS: Not entirely. The stepped forms on the façade serve as an introduction to a row of flatfront 50s speculative houses. The façade is contextual in that important sense. But it's not contextual in the sense that it mimics its neighbors or that it's constructed in a historically "correct" style for San Francisco.

WL: Do you think modernist work can convey meanings that are commonly shared? Can modernist buildings embody powerful symbols of society?

JS: Absolutely. Modernist work says a great deal about much that is positive about our time. It speaks about our relations to each other and

what we value. The detailing of modernist work, the fenestration, the spatial progression in modernist buildings, and other aspects of the work contain important statements about who we are and how we inhabit places. Good modernist work conveys as much meaning to us as earlier buildings did to their creators.

WL: In San Francisco in particular the "context" word is brought up again and again to fight growth. I think responding to it is an ongoing and very difficult challenge for architects working in a modernist idiom.

JS: That's true. But, building in the Bay Area in any manner is becoming more and more difficult. We need to pay more attention to bigger issues such as the rapid increase of population in the Bay Area. If the profession will involve itself more in these important issues we can check the ever-increasing power of design review boards, which have taken much power away from design professionals. We need to be more involved in the rapid changes here if we want to prevent design review from becoming design legislation.

Above and facing page: Shay Residence, San Francisco.

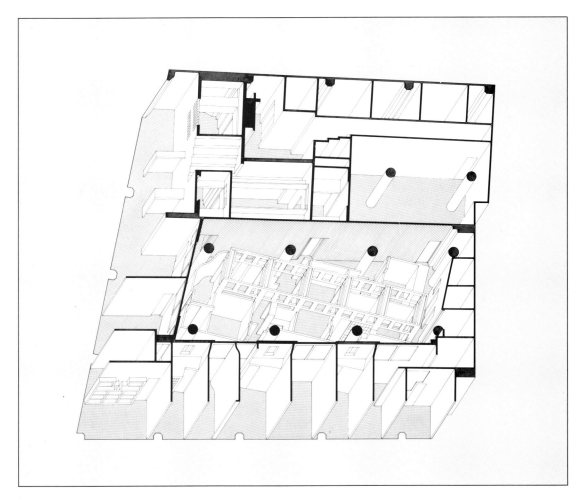

Right: Offices for Mother Jones Magazine, San Francisco.

Simon Martin–Vegue Winkelstein Moris

Cathy Simon

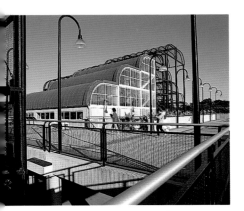

Above: Thelma B. Dolger Primate Center, San Francisco Zoo. Robert Marquis and Associates, Architects. Robert Marquis and Cathy Simon designers.

Facing page top: College Eight, University of California, Santa Cruz. Facing page bottom: Thelma B. Dolger Primate Center, San Francisco Zoo. Robert Marquis and Associates, Architects. Robert Marquis and Cathy Simon designers.

Located in San Francisco's South-of-Market area, the firm of Simon Martin–Vegue Winkelstein Moris undertakes a number of large commissions on the East and West coasts of America. Among these are the commission to design a new campus for the University of California at Santa Cruz and the design of a new sewage treatment facility for the city of San Francisco. The firm is composed of forty-five people and undertakes interior commissions as well as architectural projects.

JS: How did your partnership come about?

CS: We were five of six principals at Marquis Associates. There comes a certain point in your life where you're responsible for a tremendous amount of the work and need some recognition of that, whether it's through the name of the firm or through control of the work. For me, it was the great desire to control the design work. And that, by the way, is hard to do in some settings. For me, the creation of SMWM really had to do with being in my early 40s and feeling that I either had to make the break or I never would. It came at a very fortuitous moment for me, because the Primate Discovery Center had been personally very rewarding for me, and also had given community recognition to my work. Still, it was very hard to do, emotionally.

JS: So, everyone with their name on the door came over to the new firm?

CS: Everyone plus one. The name of the firm really came about in an effort to identify the partners, each of whom was known in the community and had a lot of good will. We were able to start our new firm with a tremendous amount of new work and community good will.

JS: How would you characterize the firm's approach to architecture?

CS: In general, I call the approach that we take to all our projects "critical contextualism." This has to do with looking at the specific issues of site and context as important points of departure for our design work.

JS: Why?

CS: Because we are urbanists, and because we believe that buildings always take their place *in relation* to other things. Most of our projects are public—for institutions or for government— and that means we're working on a site or campus with an existing fabric. Buildings can either fit into that fabric or create new places out of that fabric without violating it. "Critical contextualism" means investigating questions of site in the broadest possible sense. Not only do you analyze the physical aspects of site and proportions, materials and details used in adjacent buildings, but more abstract issues as well.

JS: How does your concern for fitting buildings into the landscape apply to the design of the new college you're doing for the University of California at Santa Cruz?

CS: The college is very much tailored to the specific landscape. The site is a south-facing hillside that slopes down and looks at the Monterey Bay. It's very Mediterranean and very beautiful. The buildings are organized in a very clear and ordered fashion within the much more informal landscape. That's not been true in previous colleges at Santa Cruz.

JS: Yes, but California architecture and planning is often characterized by a certain informality. What about Kresge College by M/L/T/W?

CS: That is a both formal and informal plan. It's very particularized. At the same time it was designed, Joseph Esherick's office did Stevenson College, which is much more simple and truly informal.

JS: So, your plan will be a contrast.

CS: Yes. It's also on a very different type of site, a meadow rather than the ecotone, the wooded forest edge. To me, a formal response was more appropriate to this setting. As they step down the hill, the buildings are visible in the meadow and have to convey the larger order of the college. The plan is very ordered and axial, based on topography, sun, and views. The landscape is integrated and more formal and, because of that, more controversial.

Skidmore Owings and Merrill

Marc Goldstein and John Kriken

The San Francisco office of Skidmore Owings and Merrill undertakes a wide variety of commissions throughout the world involving architecture, planning, and interiors. Partner Marc Goldstein has been project designer or project partner on numerous San Francisco projects, including the Bank of America World Headquarters (done as a joint venture with Wurster Bernardi and Emmons, with Pietro Belluschi as design consultant) and the recently completed 345 California Center building. John Kriken is an architect and planner. He became a partner in SOM in 1984. He currently directs the planning effort for the new Mission Bay project in San Francisco.

JS: When we think of our role in society, we must consider the impact of our work. Obviously, the highrises you design for San Francisco have an enormous impact on the city. They affect transportation, employment, the daily life that goes on around them, and a city's visual aesthetics. For some writers and critics they have become symbols of the failure of our cities, corporate greed, and other contemporary maladies, real and imagined. The list of sins architects are associated with by some writers is endless. I have seldom heard architects respond to those criticisms.

SOM: We need to think about settlement patterns and our responsibility to build cities in ways that make transportation work and in ways that allow for accessible open space. High density centers are a survival tool that permit us to structure transportation in ways that are our only hope to maintain communication between home and work. SOM builds cities. Without them there is only sprawl, chaos, waste, and pollution. One need only compare the Bay Area to settlement patterns like Houston or Los Angeles to recognize that when cities are not valued for their ability to preserve open space and reasonable commute times they become catastrophes.

We don't think young architects should be scared away from working on highrises by mongering about corporate greed. If we were in a mud-slinging frame of mind we might say, Why do people build villas in the Napa Valley? The highrise is a symbol and a villa is a symbol. In America today a person sleeping on a sidewalk is a horrible symbol. If you are involved in symbol making you should be damned aware of what you're doing and not get defensive about it.

JS: At one time highrises were seen as embodying magnificent ideals and aspirations.

Left and right: 388 Market Street, San Francisco.

SOM: They were. In the 30s there were beautiful images of ironmongers hundreds of feet in the sky leaping from beam to beam and flinging rivets through space.

JS: Wonderful black-and-white photographs.

SOM: They are wonderful. The highrise is the result of a technology which allows us to build up density where needed. As an architect you have to do it in the right place in the right time and, hopefully, give it beautiful form. Highrises shouldn't be seen as symbols of servitude to the so-called evils of capitalism or as things we need to keep our architectural children—the students—away from so that they won't be tainted. It is very important that this sort of poison not be planted. The logical conclusion to the anti-highrise train of thought is that Leonardo should not have designed fortresses.

JS: Or Michelangelo should not have worked for the Medici.

SOM: Right. There are two ways in which highrises, or high density, can abuse the environment. The first is with shadows. For many years public policy did not concern itself with casting shadows on public open space. The other is the question of compatible scale. How do we achieve transitions from, let's say, single family homes to large buildings. Today, both of these issues are well known and the problems are fewer.

But, there is another side of the highrise issue. Their real value stems from the human dimension of the areas in cities that we call downtown. Highrises stand for the importance and desirability we place on close face-to-face associations. They come from the very basic need of people to come together with some kind of reasonable transportation to and from their homes to work. Virtually all American downtowns have been built with a dimension of walking across them that is approximately twenty minutes. That's because of the need of businesses to be close to each other. In downtown San Francisco it is the desirability of these close associations that creates land value, not real estate speculation. The comparison made earlier between San Francisco and cities like Houston or Los Angeles also applies here. In those cities the kind of dynamic we are describing has not been encouraged by public policy. The resulting free-will speculation has created sprawl and many of the problems that we associate with urban living.

JS: Some of those problems exist here, though. Transportation, for one.

SOM: San Francisco is built on a peninsula of land that is surrounded by water on three sides. Regardless of any employment concentration, it will always have a transportation problem. There is a logic that suggests that San Francisco needs to control the dynamic of growth in relationship to its transportation. What we hope is that this will create a time, an historic moment for Oakland to realize its important role in the Bay Area as a place of employment. Compared to San Francisco, Oakland has far superior access.

That is the kind of settlement question that we as a firm, as individuals, and as architects need to take leadership in. It's very important that Oakland assumes increased density so that employment does not leave the region or scatter to the suburbs in sprawling industrial parks. If it doesn't assume this role and increase its density, there will be much greater transportation problems for the whole Bay Area and demands for housing in areas that otherwise would be preserved for agriculture.

JS: Do you think that within this region there is anything beyond the everpresent bay window syndrome that could generate forms for large office buildings that reflect their unique setting in the Bay Area? Are there aspects of climate, or landforms, or other things that could contribute to a regional aspect in large office buildings?

SOM: Putting aside questions of materials or visual references such as bay windows, there is no question that buildings constructed in Chicago and New York would appear crazy in this environment, by virtue of their girth and size, and because of the street widths here. Building blocks here have a much lacier or finer grain than in Chicago or New York. But, beyond this, the answer to your question is probably no. There is no regional architecture for towers, because they are more and more designed by people who don't live in the city they are to be built in. We build towers in Miami, Buffalo, and most downtowns of the United States, and other architects from across America build towers here. San Francisco has never been isolated regionally. It was never an isolated little city on the side of the Bay with some gold miners filtering in and out. Even in Gold Rush days San Franciscans would employ a Beaux Arts architect from France or New York to design a building on the top of Nob Hill. Where is the regionalism in the Pacific Union Club?

JS: Many twentieth-century planning concepts have not worked. Among them are Le Corbusier's plans for slabs of housing set in parks and Frank Lloyd Wright's agrarian communities of individual homes set in very private plots of land. These schemes embodied their creator's social values. What personal and professional values and goals are represented in your plans for the Mission Bay project in San Francisco, and why do you think the project will succeed?

SOM: The kind of modern architecture you mention had an utopian ideal that described a "brave new world" disassociated from the past. In the example of Le Corbusier, this became large, singular building projects that could be rubber-stamped over large land areas. This attitude destroyed large parts of older cities in order to put up building slabs in green parks. In contrast, we are interested in finding ways to create the variety, surprise, and interest—all the qualities of livability—that are found in the best neighborhoods of older cities. For example, in our plan for Mission Bay, buildings are addressed off small alleys and streets that bend to contain views and angle to provide glimpses of the downtown and Bay. There are a variety of small parks, as there are in many older cities, interwoven in the plan. They become surprise encounters as you pass through a neighborhood. We also believe that creating a neighborhood identity requires a clearly identified and traditional shopping street. To create this, we thought of San Francisco's Columbus Avenue and Washington Square as prototypes and borrowed from them to create Mission Bay's unique focus and place of gathering.

JS: In your planning for the project, you are in part recreating existing San Francisco typologies, such as the midblock alley.

SOM: Yes. Because we are creating an entirely new neighborhood, what we are doing is not preservation but clearly taking cues and typologies from the past. Achieving the diversity and complexity we enjoy in San Francisco neighborhoods in a new large-scale project is very, very difficult. To do this, we are planning to establish very small development increments that can be undertaken by different developers and architects to create, again, the variety, surprise, and interest found in our older cities. It's much easier to produce the modern architecture utopian ideal of Le Corbusier's.

In Mission Bay we are trying to build an urban village within the incredible dynamic of enormous political complexity and a very large financial and management responsibility. There are few precedents for this kind of project in the world.

JS: How do you respect the enormous influence of the past and environmental concerns and still produce fresh work? Some recent housing projects in the city retain a freshness and originality while fitting in. Others are so contextual they become boring.

SOM: That is precisely the challenge. Good architecture and good planning are all about working within a very demanding environment while retaining a sense of yourself as a professional who can impact a very complex process. Every problem represents a concern in some way for compatibility. But, we're not building barracks. We want each project to separate itself importantly from its background. The art is finding that balance. San Francisco, more than any other American city, has forced architects to deal first with the compatibility consideration. When doing anything in this city we must first convince people that it is respectful of its setting.

JS: It has become very important to preserve and maintain San Francisco's existing character.

SOM: The issue is larger than simply preserving buildings, open space, and street patterns. It's a mistake to limit one's thinking to the immediate future. We are committed to the broader issue of the settlement pattern of the entire Bay Area. Projects must be regarded as to what they do to transportation patterns and employment patterns. Environmental issues are global. Architects and the profession can and should play a very important role in the global process.

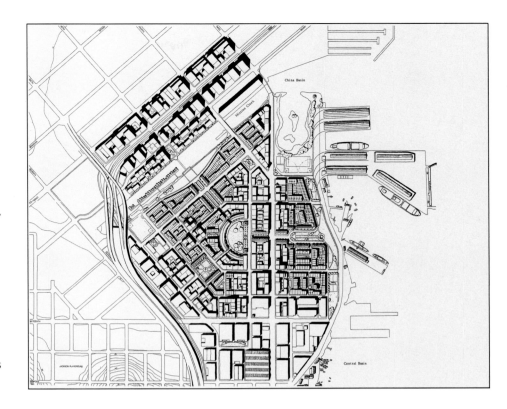

Above: site plan, Mission Bay Project, San Francisco.

JS: How does that apply in the Bay Area?

SOM: We have a critical responsibility because, of all the people who are involved in thinking about the Bay Area's future, we are the ones who can provide an image of visions about the future. We can create images that people can judge and test against their own values and aspirations. Perhaps it is a bit much to say that the architect is the conscience of the process. But, because of our training and the historic nature of the disciplines of planning and architecture, we find ourselves increasingly in this position. It is clearly the architect's role to visualize and to place alternatives on the table so that everyone is looking at the same things. We believe it is terribly important for the environmental designer to be a conscience for doing the right thing.

JS: My last question for you is about the workings of the firm. In 1975 I worked in your office in Tehran for seven months on a university project as the representative of the Mandala Collaborative, your joint-venture partner. I sat across from Rick Keating, who at that time was somewhat low on the totem pole. Fazlur Khan, who was a world-famous engineer and partner in SOM, spent a great deal of time working with Rick on the university. I admired how a senior partner would spend so much time with a young architect. That interaction took place in a small satellite office. Is it possible for young architects in Skidmore's enormous offices to work like that with more established members of the firm?

SOM: That is exactly the philosophy of the firm. The partners' role is very concerned with nurturing and bringing forward the younger people of the office. The partners are dedicated to the continuation of the firm. One of the important responsibilities is finding talent that is better than you and will eventually take your place.

New Architecture

Thomas Gordon Smith

A Bay Area native, Thomas Gordon Smith is Associate Professor of Architecture at the University of Illinois, Chicago. He revived the moribund San Francisco Architectural Club and has been, during his time in San Francisco, very active in the architectural community. He is a graduate of the University of California, Berkeley and received the Rome Prize in Architecture from the American Academy in Rome in 1979. He is completing a newly translated and illustrated edition of Vitruvius' *Ten Books on Architecture*.

JS: In your recent book, *Classical Architecture/Rule and Invention*, you talk about the Temple of Wings in Berkeley, a classical pavilion style house, and how it influenced your decision to become a classical architect. You said,

> When I first saw the Temple of Wings, it profoundly affected my sense of what architecture could be. My impressions are a synthesis of images of the house in its original state, combined with memories of the polychromed walls as they stand today. I learned that classicism did not have to be stiff and formal. I caught the living spirit of the building and the experience introduced me to the possibilities of a cultured life within the confines of a family home. It became a model for combining the intangible aspects of humanity and spirit within the "ancient" forms of classical architecture.

TGS: I was a teenager at that time, so my response was intuitive. The exposure to that building and the life that went on around it gave me an alternate view of how one might live differently from that being projected by Disney and others in the 50s who were involved in the notion of Century 21.

JS: What did you react against in the so-called idea of Century 21 and its view of the future?

TGS: I was as intrigued by it as anyone and drew designs for houses that reflected that approach, but, the Boynton house, the Temple of Wings, provided a foil and a tangible experience of the historical forms I was attracted to in books.

JS: The classicism in the Temple of Wings also embodied a way of life that went on there. What about that appealed to you?

TGS: Mrs. Quitzow, daughter of the original builder, organized parties for young people as part of her school of Isadora Duncan-style dance. The life was based upon decorum and she insisted on those values for us. The parties were extremely well organized with

Above: Tuscan House, Livermore.

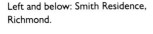

Left and below: Smith Residence, Richmond.

great understanding of what kids in their early teenage years need socially. Also, by being in that part of Berkeley I began to see Maybeck's work specifically and was very impressed by it. But it was my fantasy as a teenager that he was more overtly classical than he really is.

JS: What else influenced you toward classicism?

TGS: I spent a year in Paris as an undergraduate and made extremely extensive tours of Romanesque and Gothic buildings. I was married in 1970 and spent eight months in Europe looking at Renaissance and Baroque buildings. We lived in Vincenza for two months so that I could look at all of the Palladio and Scamozzi buildings and their antecedents from the 1400s. That prepared me for study at Berkeley, but my projects there were like Italian vernacular or overtly Prairie School. I was studying experimental monuments from the turn of the century as part of my research on Maybeck's younger contemporary, John Hudson Thomas. The choice between emulating early aspects of modernism or classical forms came during a Brunner Fellowship trip in Eastern Europe and Italy in 1976. Baroque had actually won out by then, but I looked equally at the early twentieth century. After formulating an approach to classical elements in hypothetical projects I cemented my orientation during the year in Rome at the American Academy, in 1979 and 1980.

JS: In your book you talk about creating an authentic classical architecture for our time and place. In your earlier years was there anything specifically American, as opposed to the European classical tradition and Palladio, that led you toward a contemporary classicism?

TGS: I spent a summer doing graduate school in Knoxville, Tennessee, with the Historic American Building Survey. I toured a great deal in South Carolina and Georgia and visited the antebellum houses that remain in the Piedmont region north of Atlanta. Until then I had always resisted American nineteenth-century architecture. I discovered that there was an authentic and important tradition that had been developed in specifically American forms and materials.

JS: You emphasize "authentic" architecture. In *Classical Architecture* you say that many architects speak about appropriate responses, but few speak about authenticity. I agree with you that in the 80s we hear a great deal about appropriateness but very little about authenticity. What do you mean by authentic?

TGS: A building is authentic when it responds to a commitment and belief in what is being done. That's not the only thing, though. I could simply be nostalgic about the Temple of Wings and say, Oh, that was a wonderful experience in my youth, so I'm going to do buildings that reflect it. If I never studied classicism (and by that I mean a lifetime of study), I would be tremendously limited. That's the limitation of the postmodern approach, in which there is a lack of rigor in terms of studying the paradigm and a

Above: Smith Residence, Richmond.

lack of real intention with regard to scholarship. A great deal of postmodern classicism, so-called, cannot be authentic because forms are employed with an anxiety which creates jokes or irony. It cannot have longterm impact. The most pathetic aspect of it is those big firms who have picked it up and practice it in ignorance. They use the same traits over and over.

JS: In your book why are you so hard on abstraction in twentieth-century art and architecture? What is the relevance of the forms of Doric temples over those of, say, Mies' IIT buildings, with their explicitly structural vocabulary? What is abstract about Norman Foster's work? Is complaining about this century's architecture in terms of its so-called abstraction a desire for more cultural continuity?

TGS: Although I dislike the cultural and psychological alienation that became part and parcel of modernism, I appreciate many of its expressions from the 20s through the 50s. I respond more to Le Corbusier than to Mies, but their formally abstract buildings were as parallel to the increasing hygienic preoccupations of medicine in the early century as to the car or machine. Foster may be the final chapter in this century's preoccupation with the forms of mechanical process, but probably not. The aspects I admire I see as historical phenomena. I reject the notion that its late manifestations are the only appropriate response to this time and the near future. The current and often knee-jerk rejection of classicism also rejects much else that can be part of life. In 1920 much was subverted for good reason; today the context is different.

JS: How is your work received?

TGS: The ideals of today's modernism are being laid out by people my age and younger, and what I find in them is a great intolerance. They reject classicism offhand as nostalgic without acknowledging the radical nature of the current movement. My painter friend David Ligare laughs that we are parallel to Marcel Duchamp, but our genre is no more predictable than his was in context.

JS: In doing the interviews for this book, I have encountered some hostility to your ideas.

TGS: It is important to remember that Maybeck suffered hostile and derisive comments throughout his years in San Francisco. Perhaps it is overidentification on my part, but I find that some consolation. The current hostility is certainly not confined to the Bay Area nor to me. A comment typical in its arrogance is, I've thought long and hard about this and there is no place for classicism in the future. To me that is the ultimate abstraction; neither allowing relation to the past nor admitting the life-giving potential of classical forms. It is important to emphasize that I'm not just objecting to one side of this issue.

A similar kind of intolerance toward development occurs within the practice of classicism. The English architect Quinlan Terry does not seem open to developing a new architecture. By repeating eighteenth-century theories of the origin of classical forms as though they are his and by excluding what has actually been discovered about this in recent years, he does not theorize from a contemporary position. I think Terry's buildings actually convey an almost abstract postmodern quality, but his program seems opposite that of Charles Moore. By limiting himself to a tight eighteenth-century paradigm, Terry gets close to doing something that is actually impossible—getting stuck in the past.

JS: But contemporary architects reacting against your work are thoroughly schooled in the modern movement of the twentieth century, and that includes a strong break with the past, especially classical forms. That breaking with classicism has strong moral underpinnings.

TGS: We have not undergone systems of classical instructions. In my generation, we probably felt the completeness of modernism's break with historical form during the 50s and 60s most of all. Joe Esherick, of course, had exposure to the Beaux Arts system. I feel grateful for not being trained within an established system, although

I have been building systematic teaching methods for a literate classicism over the past four years. Rather than rebuilding, Terry and others rely on an overly restrictive, "ready-made" system. We must rebuild understanding and methods by learning from the examples of spiritual mentors. Perhaps I'm seeming intolerant myself; it's just that I aim at a synthesis that draws from vast periods of time versus a more definite historical context. I probably share many basic convictions with Terry that would distinguish us from the neomoderns, but at the same time mistrust the tinges of their reactionary aspects.

It is clear that neither Terry nor I are isolated and eccentric figures. With others of our age, we are joined by many younger architects dedicated to the revival of classical forms integrated with a similar outlook on spiritual and cultural issues.

I am passionate about paradigms and in my current work on Vitruvius welcome the chance to study and learn more about my discipline. I am ultimately interested, however, in the present and am not motivated to nostalgically re-present the past.

Below: Tuscan House, Livermore.

Daniel Solomon and Associates

Daniel Solomon

Architect Daniel Solomon, recipient of over thirty awards from professional institutes and *Progressive Architecture* magazine, is in charge of planning the housing component for the Mission Bay project, a large new neighborhood to be privately developed in San Francisco. In addition to his day-to-day practice, he is a professor of architecture at the University of California at Berkeley and has lectured and published widely. He has practiced for many years from his office on Vandewater Street in San Francisco's North Beach.

JS: For whom did you design the Potrero Hill house?

DS: It's for a very interesting couple who are well-known musicians. He is the composer Pat Gleeson, who does work for the movies. She is Joan Jeanrenaud, who is the cellist of the Kronos Quartet.

JS: Are the two strangely shaped rooms in the back of the house shaped that way for acoustics?

DS: Yes, they are. One is a studio for the quartet and the other is a studio for the composer. There are two things that shape the house. One is the set of acoustic considerations that shaped the back. The other is an odd set of deed restrictions related to views from surrounding windows which determined plate heights, roof pitches, and how the house is placed on the site. The shallow roof pitch is a response to those restrictions.

JS: Why is the house black?

DS: They both had a desire for something strong, harsh, and unhouselike, and for something that was, in a way, a kind of antibourgeois bourgeois house.

JS: The small windows on the front elevation render the building scaleless.

DS: That is very deliberate. I've done a lot of tiny buildings, and one of the ways I've discovered of giving a little building presence is by making the scale ambiguous. When you have a recognizable scale established by things like doorknobs, handrail heights, and floor to floor heights, the possibility of a tiny building having a monumental presence disappears. The ambiguity of scale, which this thing has, gives it a certain strength. The two devices that contribute most strongly to that ambiguity in this building are the unity of material and the funny little windows.

JS: When I first saw it, I thought that the façade was a reflection of the highrises to the north of Potrero Hill, the grid of their elevations and their vertical massing.

Left facing page and right, top and bottom:: Gleeson-Jeanrenaud residence, San Francisco.

DS: That's an interesting thought. That hadn't occurred to me. The other thing about the materials and the whole character of the building is that it is also related to the general funkiness of Potrero Hill, particularly going east, and the ragtag industrial ad hoc house character which is very unlike the rest of the city. Most of the buildings in the rest of the city are very polite, because the rest of the city is more polite.

JS: I think the Lem House you designed in Presidio Heights is very polite. How did you derive the elevation?

DS: It's about the context in the sense that it is a frontal, central, neoclassical elevation on a San Francisco street. It's different from the typical language of the San Francisco street façades. It's flat, and has a distortion of scale with the big window. What I was interested in was having a very complex interior with a face on it which was sufficiently transparent to allow the complexity to be seen on the outside. One of the devices that allows that is putting skylights deep in the plan that make the big window transparent from outside and helps provide glimpses of all this spatial monkey business.

JS: Isn't it like being in a fishbowl inside the house?

DS: No. The head heights and sill heights as well as the areas of clear glass versus the translucent glass are all carefully adjusted so you can walk around the house and not feel like you're in a fishbowl. You really don't feel unprivate in that house.

JS: And what is the context of the San Jose housing project?

DS: It's in downtown San Jose. There is an old square, sort of an Olmstedian little park within the old grid. There are a number of handsome twenties and teens buildings on the square. Our building fills a missing tooth in this collection of public buildings.

JS: The Armancio Ergina project in San Francisco's Western Addition is low-income housing?

DS: Yes. There had been a previous design for that project, which was originally a HUD Section 8 subsidized rental project. It was designed for an entirely different program from the one it was intended to go ahead as, which was a low- and moderate-income cooperative. Also, the neighborhood had changed in the intervening years. There had been a lot of restoration and small-scale infill, which had created a partially gentrified neighborhood. The first design looked like three freestanding apartment blocks and parking lots in San Leandro. There was absolutely zero relationship to San Francisco building patterns. It was a parking lot with three dopey looking buildings in it, and was discarded on urban design grounds and grounds of safety.

JS: I read that when you took over the job there was a very limited time to do the project.

DS: There was financing attached to that project with an expiration date. Working back from the expiration date of the financing the last unit had to be through escrow in nineteen months, or some incredible time period. The bonds had an expiration date, and there was a date at which the whole thing would turn into a pumpkin. Working backwards from that we had five months from the first time I ever saw the site to get it under construction. The schedule was such that schematics were done between Thursday and Monday and never changed. That was it. It was just the most tense, hysterical and difficult time. The atmosphere of the construction trailer was like, if you remember, the inside of the submarine in *Run Silent, Run Deep*.

JS: Did you write guidelines for the San Francisco Planning Code?

DS: Yes, I've done a lot of work for the city over a period of years beginning in 1975. We're still working with the city, on the design controls for the housing component for the Mission Bay project. Prior to that we did housing standards for the South of Market Special Zoning District, a plan for Rincon Hill, and a revision for the planning code called "Change Without Loss," which was the basis of the generation of planning revisions done from 1975 to 1978. Some of those revisions were passed and others were not. After they were passed, the enforcement was so haphazard that the current effort really redoes a lot we did ten years ago that has since slipped from the code or the enforcement of the code.

JS: With the numerous planning code requirements, how do we avoid becoming overly contextual? What do you think the role of the avant-garde is with regard to building design in San Francisco?

DS: I think it's very tough. I've had the two best buildings I've ever designed in San Francisco killed by the Planning Commission. One of them was on Union Street and one was for the Winterland site in the upper Fillmore area. They weren't sufficiently straight kitsch Victorian copies. Those two were real disasters.

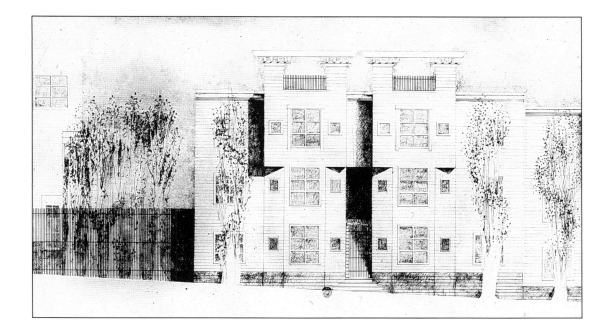

JS: San Francisco has fine examples of many periods of architecture, besides Victorian. Among all of them do you think there is anything that begins to coalesce into anything you might call uniquely San Franciscan?

DS: Well, I think San Francisco has two components. One is typological, that is, the building types that evolved out of the planning grid, which begins with the 25-foot lots the city is laid out on. That's overlaid by a series of patterns, one of which is the Tandem House, where people build small cottages on the rear of lots and big houses on the front of the lots at a later date, with a courtyard in between. This is my whole spiel about the Mission Bay plan. The courtyard typology is something that has generated a lot of very nice buildings on Russian Hill, in North Beach, and various places. One of the achievements of the 1975 to 1978 work on the planning code was a loosening up of the code to permit a historic type to be revived.

JS: The courtyard type?

DS: Yes. Projects we have done, such as the Pacific Heights Townhouses, Castro Commons, and the Midway Terrace Condominiums replicate the nineteenth-century pattern of the courtyard. So, the 25-foot grid, the courtyard, and the midblock alley, which is a speculator's pattern, are very dominant components of the San Francisco building types. They are really essential things of the urban structure of the town and are what I think all of the projects we have done in the city attempt to rediscover, reinterpret, and reinforce in one way or another. The Mission Bay plan takes the three patterns, plus another, which comes from the Marina and has apartment buildings on the corners and row houses in the midblocks. We use those patterns of historic urban structure as the basis for the planning of the 700 units of housing for Mission Bay.

JS: How did the vocabulary of your work in the 80s come about?

DS: Well, I think Ken Frampton put it very well. One night I think he had had a lot to drink and said that the difficulty architects face in the 80s, or something to that effect, is navigating between the Scylla of uninflected modernism and the Charybdis of historicist kitsch. I thought that was funny, but also very true.

I think the tension between context and the logic and rationality of the modernist dwelling is very interesting. What I hope our buildings portray is something about that tension. On the one hand there are things that are extremely antiurban and came out of a generation of antiurban buildings that had a strong emphasis on the desire for sunlight, a certain kind of relationship to the outdoors, and a whole set of values that reflected suburban life, which are opposed to things like historic continuity and the recognition of the typological order of surrounding buildings. I think my main interest is a kind of dialectic between the private and public, and the suburban and urban.

William Stout Associates

Global Architecture publications in Japan recently recognized William Stout as a member of what it calls the Emerging Generation in America, a group composed of twenty individuals and firms throughout the country practicing high-quality architecture. An active member of San Francisco's design community, he also owns William Stout Architectural Books, a large purveyor of books and publications to the Bay Area's design professionals.

JS: Your designs for the house in the wine country near Healdsburg and the Coles and Pando House in San Francisco seem quite different.

WS: That is because they are seven or eight years apart and because each time I get a project the approach is somewhat intuitive. The strength in the buildings comes from the fact that they are based on modernist ideas, and because I try to push them, which creates a lot of forcing together and clashing of modernist tendencies.

JS: What do you think you're pushing on the Healdsburg house?

WS: I think that's pretty easy to see. It's the whole idea of site. My clients wanted an indoor-outdoor house. I tried to relate the house to the ground. In fact, there are three different types of foundations in the house to deal with that concern. The slab on grade foundation was not a good idea as far as the soil there is concerned, but it provides a flat intersection with the ground. There is another situation in the Healdsburg house that I think is really interesting—how the view axis in the house sets up as you move through the space.

JS: Do you mean in the way that your eye gets turned into the courtyard and then into the central space in the house, near the stair?

WS: No. I mean that as you enter the building from the courtyard your eye goes directly out to the vineyards, so that as you transcend into the space and go through each layer your eye has different directions to go. For example, as you go into the first five-foot module after the entryway your eye transfers to the courtyard on the left. Then, as you go five more feet your eye transfers to the olive trees on the right. It probably should have been much stronger. The ideas I'm trying to do in abstraction get watered down in the reality of the program.

JS: I think that happens for most of us.

WS: Some people are able to do it. That's the nice thing about the Japanese architect Tadao Ando. He limits his palette and doesn't deal with the program.

JS: In general, what besides the modern movement in architecture influences your work?

WS: I thought about that a lot since we talked the other day. Well, not a lot, maybe fifteen minutes before you showed up tonight. I think most of my work stems from an artistic attitude toward the work and art in general, in particular the abstract expressionists such as Franz Kline, Jackson Pollock, and Ad Reinhardt. Also, some painters of the cubist era, such as Fernand Léger. I was always responsive to Michael Graves' early work, which had some of that spirit, because I thought it was really phenomenal. His work really bothers me now, because he left a modernist eclectic way of working and became just a kind of facial architect. I feel what his work lacks now is the idea of working with space, the development of it, and the perception of it as you move through it.

JS: You mention being influenced by the abstract expressionists, and the cubists, such as Braque, Picasso, and Léger. How?

WS: Well, let's say that with the abstract expressionists it is just my love of that movement, the excitement of it. The love of the cubists is really a study of line. I've been influenced for years by the study of line, the idea of it, and the idea of diagram. It's interesting, because I've been reading about a maze recently constructed near San Francisco open to the public. I want to go there. The interesting thing I've been dealing with in art is the idea of how to draw line, and what line does in two dimensions. So, I've used a lot of line images in producing my work.

The thing is, what I'm all about is a state of confusion, because it's basically a part of family life in America—the idea of moving around a lot, the idea of not being stable, and the instability of modern life. I think that shows a lot in my work, and the work is very modern in that attitude. It's not the way I want to work, but it's the way my psyche has allowed me to do it. My whole approach to architecture is process, and the idea of hardly ever going into a project with a preconceived idea. For me the process is one of finding and developing something in a client that is unique, and trying to stretch it further than they can comprehend.

JS: Your Coles and Pando House in San Francisco seems to have some of the attributes of cubist composition from Léger's paintings.

WS: What I was trying to do in that house is develop a very rational skin and a very free plan. Not freeform, but organized as a free plan. I wanted to make three houses without using bay windows, with penetrations that made the houses interesting, but allowed them to be flat. I wanted a series of flat façades with courtyards inside, somewhat similar to the later design for the Healdsburg house. As you go through the house

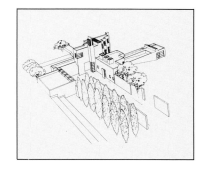

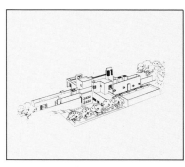

Above top and bottom: perspective view, Healdsburg house, Alexander Valley.

Left: Coles and Pando Residence, San Francisco.

on the circulation spine, the line of movement through the house, the transformation of the space occurs as you hit different points. In other words, in the Manchester Street House, as you walk through, beginning on the first level, you pass a courtyard on the left, which is the dining courtyard for the kitchen. This sets up as an outdoor transition. At that point there are no windows on the right-hand wall, so you are forced to look in the other direction. It's interesting, because there are a lot of things that happen in my houses that people wouldn't think of as houselike. I think that's good. I don't try to make my houses comfortable.

JS: You must not feel much in common with the basic Bay Area brown-shingled home. Your work is so far removed from that vision of domesticity that I don't think there is any connection.

Above: Coles and Pando Residence, San Francisco.

WS: I've never had a connection with that. I've never wanted to live in that kind of a house. To me, it's not modern. And modern to me is probably the feeling of what modernism was a hundred years ago, because it never really developed in northern California. I grew up in Idaho and never got to see much modern architecture, but I read a lot of books and looked at a lot of things. What I liked the most then is what I want to do now, and that's clean lines and the ability to not have the architecture and the detail override your feeling of the space. The space is the element you deal with.

JS: How does your process for designing a house start?

WS: I think the idea of architecture in some ways is really organizing the program, so that just before it seems organized you screw it up. Because that seems like the way my life works. In other words, you get to a certain point, and then—and I don't know if it's a matter of losing interest, or what—you arrive at a situation where you feel that maybe the conceptual ideas don't come across strongly enough, so you screw it up in some fashion.

JS: Right. I think you can see that in a lot of creative work. I mean, it's like Braque and Picasso.

WS: I look at myself and feel that I don't force my edge, although in comparison to what the norm is there may be some edging going on. I think that's why I feel very comfortable about the space below the bookstore that I designed and built to be my own office. If I had enough money to air-condition it properly it could be a fantastic space. I spent almost a year thinking about the damned thing, because I had the space and I lived in it for almost two years. I originally wanted to do something modular that was very rational and allowed the walls to be taken apart, to do something really creative in terms of form, because I'm really interested in the transformation of form and how that makes space.

JS: Regionalism is much in vogue today, and the case is made that it is in vogue because of the excesses of the International Style and its non–place-specific nature. Everyone talks about context. What do you think of that?

WS: That's what I like about the original modernist work, that it is not place-specific.

JS: That's refreshing. You like it because it's *not* place-specific.

WS: Absolutely. What I feel was breaking down in that period were the regionalist styles as the ability to communicate and travel between cultures increased. That's basically what most people don't like. They feel they lose their identity. I think what happened in architecture is that people weren't able to take those changes and use them to make individual work within the modernist format. But, any good piece of architecture has to deal with all of its surroundings. If you're doing bay windows in the Bay Area, you can reassess what the bay window is. A bay window doesn't have to be at 45 degrees to the façade just because the planning department says so.

JS: A great bay window is on the northwest corner of one the finest modernist houses in San Francisco, the Russell House by Eric Mendelsohn.

Who would you name as someone you admire in architecture?

WS: Carlo Scarpa. I mean, I liked him before anybody knew who he was. I never really thought of him as an architect, and I think of myself a little in that manner. If I can keep going for forty or fifty years I might very well be at the same level that he was. He wasn't just an architect, and didn't do any architecture much of his life. He was interested in a whole range of things.

JS: He didn't do much building.

WS: Very little, but I think he was pretty happy with his life.

JS: Do you think he went home at night and beat his head against the wall because he didn't have more work?

WS: I don't think so. I'm sure he had a dilemma about it, but I don't think he could have handled the work anyway. I think we are who we want to be.

Right and below: Coles and Pando
Residence, San Francisco.

Paulett Taggart Architects

Paulett Taggart

Paulett Taggart began her independent practice as an architect in 1987 in San Francisco after many years of working for some of the Bay Area's finest architects. During the time she worked for Daniel Solomon Associates, she contributed greatly to the design of the Castro Commons condominium project, a San Francisco development designed specifically for clients with nontraditional lifestyles. A graduate of the University of Oregon and the Harvard Graduate School of Design, she is active in the local design community. Her current practice includes a variety of commissions for residential and commercial clients.

JS: What is the size and layout of the Heinemann/ Kueffner remodel?

PT: The building is 20 feet by 54 feet. The area for their unit is a floor and a half, so you can see that a part of the challenge here was to make the place feel more spacious than it really is. The living spaces themselves were all right in terms of location so that the main design problem became creating the stairway. The stair became the problem and the opportunity. It not only organizes and connects the four levels (entry, sleeping, living, and roof room/deck) but it introduces a dynamic vertical light shaft, balancing the light in all the rooms and giving the house a powerful sense of space without giving up square footage.

JS: And why did you go without trim?

PT: I was trying to achieve a continuity of space and a connection between each living area and the vertical stair space that connects them all. The unit is small enough that even a detail like trim has the effect of breaking the continuity of a space. I eliminated the trim to allow the space to flow and used only soffits to help define the rooms.

JS: Why do you work in a minimalist vein?

PT: That's a good question. Because I like it.

JS: That's a good answer.

PT: Actually, the character of my work varies to some extent depending on the client. My clients for the 1236 Montgomery remodel were great in encouraging me to push the minimalist edge. I've had many clients who needed something softer; who can't handle the hard-edged minimalism. On that project the aesthetic is a combination of my design approach and a desire to experiment with materials like steel, block, and cable, along with the clients' aesthetic which strongly supported that approach. I have other jobs where it is much more difficult to reconcile the clients' more traditional taste with what works for me ideologically.

JS: So for you it is an ideological question?

PT: Yes. I just can't do it any other way. There is a range in my approach but there is only one approach. I think my range is fairly broad in terms of how far I can go in working with a traditional style, particularly when it involves working with an existing building, but there are limits. We all run into that.

I do not see my approach to design as a style. I don't see it as simply form follows function either, but I find the seed for my design ideas in the problems that need to be resolved. There is frequently some strong underlying need or desire that helps to set the artistic direction and helps to form the design idea. In the Holcomb Print Shop, for instance, I was designing a workspace for a letterpress printer. The building's concrete structure and brick infill left no way to hide the power we needed to run the four presses, as well as lighting, phones, and outlets. I took that opportunity to develop a framework for the space out of inexpensive channel framing which is the electrical conduit but becomes a sort of minimalist sculpture. These repeated elements help organize and unify the four distinct bays of the printshop and stand as a counterpoint to the rough and massive concrete. So the resolution of one of the design problems became the seed of the concept for the design solution.

JS: But it often seems to me that when we make the leap from figuring out the problem diagrammatically to creating form, what many modernists are really practicing is a kind of hybrid functionalism. The case can be made that however elegant the results, they may be seen in their reductive way as very restrained expressions of what architecture can be.

PT: I don't see my approach to design as a straight 60s form follows function. I see the functional aspects as providing opportunities to find a kernel that can develop into the design concept which can then be developed into the expression of the building. I think much of the ornament and embellishment on buildings gives one the sense that it was stuck on as an afterthought rather than that it has to do with the idea of the building. That it comes from within.

JS: How about the embellishment on a Sullivan building or an Eliel Saarinan building? And what about the more contemporary idea of collaging elements onto a façade or interior?

PT: There are many ways to embellish a building. My concern is that the embellishment have a *raison d'être*; that each part has a relationship to the whole, and a contribution to make to the whole. The ornament I dislike is ornament for ornament's sake.

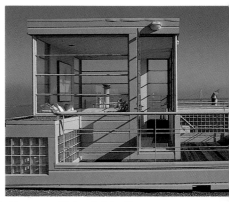

Above, top: Holcomb Print Shop, San Francisco. Above, bottom: Heinemann/Kueffner Residence, San Francisco.

Left: Heinemann/Kueffner Residence, San Francisco.

Tai Associates

Vincent Tai

 In addition to projects done for clients, the firm of Tai Associates designs projects in which Vincent Tai is the developer. This has resulted in an architectural office that has a very good understanding of the many aspects of development. A native of Hong Kong, Vincent Tai practices architecture from a renovated three-story structure in San Francisco's North Beach. The firm's designs have been recognized with a Progressive Architecture Award and a San Francisco Institute of Architects Merit Award for architectural design.

JS: On Front Street, if I'm clear, the problem was to design a building that would fit the planning envelope and be somehow or another historically correct.

VT: We picked the vocabulary of the building from the previous four-story building on the site, which we demolished. Because we're in a historical district we had to appear before the Landmark Board. In San Francisco there are historic districts that require very thoughtful adaptations of new buildings to what is already in place, so we made it easy to sell. Our intent, though, was not to directly copy the past but to use the original building as a guideline to assist us in coming up with a modern structure.

The project, in a way, is the combination of many impossibilities that resolve themselves. We had two very good clients, two brothers, originally from Hong Kong. The building was built to honor their great-grandfather, who was a very well-known figure in Southeast Asia. They questioned the two pairs of steel columns at the entrance. Their father, who lives in Hong Kong, didn't think that they were necessary and appropriate. So what we have done is to provide removable columns. If the father comes to town and doesn't like them, we will take them out. When he goes back to Hong Kong, we will put them back on the façade.

JS: I think you need them, because the front of the building is articulated, it seems to me, to express all the steel we need to put in brick buildings to make them earthquake safe. You've poetically exposed the steel rather than hid it or simply put up some dumb-looking cross-braces, such as one sees in many new and renovated structures throughout town. In doing that, though, you've stretched the paradox, or the enigma, of how the building is seen. I mean, is it old-old, or new-old, or added-to, or what?

VT: That was not the intent, to articulate the steel structure, but now that you mention it, it does look that way. In fact, I have had people think it was an old building being renovated.

JS: I want to ask you about the project you did at Second and Harrison. I liked the original design very much, but what is being built there looks like an extremely watered-down version of the original. What happened?

VT: The developer we did the project for sold the land to another developer, who hired another architect, who, I guess you could say, drastically changed it.

JS: Your original design very nicely picked up the forms of the adjacent coffee company building. The forms you used seemed to have a particular relevance to the site, and the scale and materials were just right. It seemed like an excellent solution to the problem of building in a city with such high regard for its old buildings. What was finally built there seems to have lifted your building's appearance a bit, but none of the concepts, so that the design, which was so interesting, has lost all its strength. Did you have any trouble getting your original design through city planning?

VT: Oh, no, we got it through the first time. They really liked it. But, we sometimes have a lot of problems with the planning staff. Not because they are not cooperative enough, or are not good designers, but because they all have different ideas. And, to me they are a quasi-political body, because they have to keep the neighbors happy. The neighborhood groups have their own good reasons for the protection of their lifestyles in San Francisco. Unfortunately, they are all using, let's call it contextual patterning, as one of the many ways for them to kill a project as proposed. So, the first thing we do in San Francisco is to appropriately scale the building. Another problem is the San Francisco Planning Code, which really only works as a reference test, because it is constantly being revised, and because the final judgment on a project is based on discretion rather than the planning rules. After you have a chance to look through the planning code you should throw it out the window. We have been told on some projects to follow the next code regulations coming up, even though they have not yet had a public hearing. Of course the planners are doing us a favor by letting us know, but it's still a difficult situation for a developer to be in.

Left: Front Street Office Building, San Francisco.

Right: Harrison Street Office Building, San Francisco.

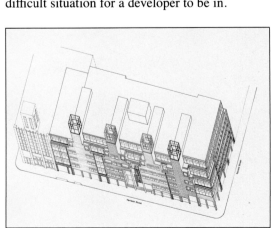

Tanner Leddy Maytum Stacy

(formerly Tanner and VanDine)
William Leddy

 Recipient of two San Francisco AIA design awards for interior projects in 1988, the firm of Tanner Leddy Maytum Stacy, formerly known as Tanner and VanDine, practices from their newly renovated offices directly under the San Francisco end of the Bay Bridge. Four partners direct the firm. They are James L. Tanner, William Leddy, Marsha Maytum, and Richard Stacy. Founding partner Peter Van-Dine left the firm in 1988 to pursue other interests in architecture. The work of the firm is modernist and includes projects such as San Francisco's Jewelry Mart, a large building wrapped in glass block, and a new highrise hotel for San Diego.

JS: The spaces in the loft remodel have a strongly abstract, almost diagrammatic clarity. I wonder how you derived them, and what led you to such a straightforward, almost industrial, use of materials.

Above: Studio/Residence, San Francisco.

Top and bottom left: Studio/ Residence, San Francisco.

WL: The building was generated by circumstance, function, and poetic intent. The program we received from the client was very specific and almost suburban in character, with two major exceptions: They needed a large painting studio capable of accommodating very large canvases, and they wanted to fit the entire house within an old industrial building located in a very dense part of San Francisco's North Beach. The decision to put the studio in the back, away from the street, seemed to be an obvious solution. It began to create a very linear diagram because of the need to get large paintings from the studio to the street. The tall, vertical slots in the courtyard are there to allow the passage of the paintings to the outside. The courtyard in the middle of the house is for light and air, so the house became very internalized.

The project's detailing and construction grew out of our desire to respect the existing volume and its three bowstring trusses spanning the space and use them as the ribs of a carcass into which the elements of the building's new life would be inserted. To accomplish this, the upper floors were treated as independent elements standing free of the side walls and the trusses, and attaching themselves to the existing shell only at the roof. The result is that the preexisting structural order of the building is revealed progressively as one moves through the spaces. The first truss emerges from between two walls at the second floor, the second crashes across the interior courtyard, and the third stands fully revealed in the rear studio. We wanted the house to tell its story in a very clear and straightforward way.

JS: You used the introduction of light and air into the space as a way of generating architectural volumes, which became the negative spaces in a compositional sense, not used for strictly programmed areas.

WL: Right. We pulled the new elements away from the sidewalls, which were a reference point of existing work, and allowed light down between the cracks into the first-floor spaces. And the central courtyard was designed as a completely open glass cage, intended to fill the middle of the house with light. The configuration of spaces is partially a result of reaching for light on a very constricted site.

JS: Why did you use aluminum in the courtyard?

WL: It was cheap and steel was prohibitively expensive. I think all the materials in the building look simple. For example, the aluminum grating on the second-floor landing sits on unfinished wood joists.

JS: I think the wood floors keep the project from becoming visually cold.

WL: Yes, but you can always add rugs and paintings. I always thought of the work as a sort of baggy overcoat—it just sort of fits.

JS: I think it's more like a good suit.

WL: Well, I think it's a baggy overcoat in that the main space is generalized and can be perceived and occupied in a number of different ways.

JS: It's a very clear building with a straightforward plan and volumetric relationships. Would you say you like a reductivist approach?

WL: Reductivism is more than an aesthetic preference, although that's certainly part of it. For us, it's a way of expressing the essential meaning of a building in clear, understandable language. It's a language that isn't necessarily culturally derived, but one which tries to address the basic nature of things in a way which will heighten the experience of a place. We live in a very complex society, and I think to be able to walk into a space that is clearly derived and that has light washing its walls and hopefully some kind of nature to be viewed is very comforting. This is like Hiroshi Hara's early work. He did a series of houses that are very internalized and top-lit.

JS: You think that our time is somehow more difficult to cope with than earlier decades, or centuries?

WL: Finding moments of repose is more difficult, particularly in urban residential architecture.

JS: Do you think the forms of this project visually relate to other Bay Area architecture?

WL: No, except that its proportions are derived from a tight urban setting. This particular building responds to very specific localized circumstances, which are existing structure, volume, light, function, the density of its block. It doesn't try to be anything other than what it is.

I don't think there is a regional style today in the Bay Area. Perhaps one existed at the turn of the century when technologies and cultural viewpoints were fairly isolated and distinct, but information is so quickly disseminated today that many of those distinctions have, unfortunately, fallen away.

JS: Do you think that there are enough unique influences in San Francisco—such as the many overcast and cloudy days, the seismic problem, the standardized lot widths, and perhaps even the local building vernacular—to create, at least in local, contemporary residential architecture many common characteristics of form?

WL: I think we would all like to think that our particular response to architecture is unique to ourselves and our own area or setting. But good design derives its uniqueness from an honest response to real circumstances at hand, many of which you've mentioned—climate, topography, urban density—not from a quasiromantic notion of what buildings should look like. As an example, bay windows make a certain amount of sense in San Francisco because they provide a way of expanding the building beyond constricted property lines, while also grabbing more light into long, dark interiors. This doesn't mean they necessarily have to have 45 degree sides or double-hung windows to be successful or meaningful. There are any number of ways to do a good bay window. The net result of many such specific responses in localized areas might result in neighboring buildings that share some similarities; I don't know whether that would make it a style.

JS: Perhaps attempts to create a regional style are a longing for whatever it was that was good in earlier, more isolated times. Maybe we need to see in our buildings and way of dressing, perhaps even our languages or dialects, something strongly different about ourselves compared to others. It could be that the International Style came up very short there. What do you think?

WL: Obviously, the increasing standardization of the physical environment is disturbing, and we should strive to accentuate those aspects of life that make us unique. But, this should be done in a meaningful way, responding to the essential realities of a place, in straightforward and significant ways. When a particular style is anointed as being regional, the end result too often seems to be a suppression of new ways of doing things. All of a sudden, every new house in San Francisco has to be fake Victorian, every new house in Berkeley has to be fake Maybeck.

JS: How would you describe your approach to architecture?

WL: For us, making architecture isn't pure heroic creation. It's sweaty business. It has to do with going through the functional requirements, the codes, the detailing, materials and structure—all the nitty-gritty elements of architecture—to find the poetry.

Right and bottom: Offices of Tanner Leddy Maytum Stacy, San Francisco.

Below: Drypolcher Residence, San Francisco.

William Turnbull Associates

William Turnbull

 Internationally renowned architect William Turnbull was a founder, with Charles Moore, Donlyn Lyndon and Richard Whittaker, of the highly influential M/L/T/W Architects, which practiced as a group in the Bay Area during the 60s. Now practicing independently from his office on Pier 1½ in San Francisco, he designs a variety of commissions worldwide. He coauthored *The Place of Houses*, published in 1979. It presents attitudes about housing that he shares with coauthors Moore, Lyndon, and Gerald Allen. He has received numerous professional awards and has been a Fellow of the American Academy in Rome.

JS: Does the traditional aspect of your recent buildings in the Napa Valley indicate a shift in your philosophy about the forms of building in general, or is it a particular response to the setting?

WT: It is a particular response to Napa. Like a Napa Valley barn, the Spencer House is a simple big-roofed structure, rectangular in plan. The house under the roof cuts in and out, responding to living patterns. The roof defines the space between the inside and outside, a pragmatic layer that shields the sun in the summertime and provides a place for people to sit. The roof acts as a parasol, and the framing is exposed the way it is on a parasol. So, the house does look deceptively like a traditional house. The best thing about it is that it is not a "look-at-me, look-at-me" house. The house creates a special retreat for a private family in the middle of the Napa Valley tourist world. No tourists pull off to look at it. That's good.

JS: I've looked at the plans of many of your houses, and they all have a remarkably idiosyncratic nature to them. They're extremely playful and clever. The Napa buildings in particular seem to be a strong contrast to the work in the same area by architects strongly influenced by rationalism who try to cut out a lot of the idiosyncratic from their buildings.

WT: I don't think it is good to do that. The rationalist buildings lack joy or delight. They are well crafted, but heavy footed. Houses should represent what makes each of us unique. When I talk to clients I try to smoke out their dreams and desires, to figure out what makes each client different from someone else. For example, you may have wanted a tree house since you were four, and it will take me awhile to find that out. Everybody has secret dreams, and building a house explores them.

JS: Do you get your information from interviews, or do you also use the checklist in *The Place of Houses*?

Left and right: Private residence, Napa Valley.

WT: I never formalize it. I sit and talk with the client. The checklist is useful for the client to organize his needs, but I design in metaphors. What does a building want to be like? So, the metaphor for the Spencer House became a parasol to keep off the sun.

JS: Can you put into words what values your buildings represent?

WT: When asked what guides my work I would answer—the people and the landscape. Building something is a mutual adventure. I bring certain things to the process as a professional, but the owner brings the hopes and dreams. The trick is to marry up who the client is with the program and the budget. Some people cannot talk about what they want.

JS: What do you do then?

WT: I talk to the site. There are two sources for inspiration on any residential problem: the individual and his idiosyncrasies, and the site. I listen to both.

JS: There is a recurring motif in your recent work of the octagonal tower and the large sheltering roof. What is the importance to you of these forms?

WT: Octagons are an anchoring geometry. In the American Club in Hong Kong, it ties the building to the landscape the same way a lighthouse sits on a rocky site. At the Mountain View Civic Center, two octagons form a gateway between the urban world of the major downtown street and the park. They function as a spatial marker and an anchor. Recently, the octagon form has been of interest to me, but it is only an idea that has worked itself into projects and will work its way out again. Occasionally as I work I discover design elements that can be used in different ways. In the 60s, we did a series of what I call wall houses. We took the wall, opened it up, and hung saddlebags on it. It was an interesting idea at the time, and we played with it for three or four years.

JS: That idea, of hanging saddlebags onto the wall, is reminiscent of your great teacher, Louis Kahn, and his thoughts about servant and served spaces. Are there ideas of his that are still playing themselves out in your work in the 80s?

WT: Kahn was very tough in terms of one's visual vocabulary. I had a roommate who did a high school for his thesis with some of Kahn's forms. I can still remember that critique. Kahn spent two hours tearing him to pieces and shredding his project. Kahn insisted that you find your own forms and way of making a personal architecture.

What is retained from the Kahn years is the desire for excellence, a standard that is hard to consistently live up to. Kahn set a standard, and I have spent thirty years attempting to come somewhere near what he demanded. It is the standard of excellence holding the notion that a building is not worth doing unless it has its own specific ideas. The formalism of Kahn's own vocabulary, his fingerprint, was never an issue in discussions about good design.

JS: You were in school during the end of a great period of modernism and began your career not too long before the advent of postmodernism. Yet your work is never characterized by either a hardedged kind of modernity, nor does it take forms from the architectural past.

WT: When I went to school, we started by designing Mies van der Rohe–derived projects. The style was not important. We learned there was a great architectural history that preceded Mies, and the direction was to look at the past in terms of its lessons, not to make the mistake of many recent architects who recall specifically the forms of the past, of Rome, or of Luytens. Look at the past, for the lessons, not for the specifics. It is the principle of creative forgetfulness.

For me the land and the landscape is a great catalyst. I try to knit buildings into the land in ways that enhance the quality of the existing site, in contrast to the modernist approach of dropping something gracefully and gently onto it. In the Villa Savoye or the Farnsworth House, you are apart from the landscape, you are utopian, a materialist, and everything is detailed as though the land is like so much sand. That attitude says if you touch the land it will yield and isn't important, that what is important is the ship on top of it. I am more from a background attuned to the Wrightian point of view of integrating construction with the landscape.

JS: Why is that?

WT: I grew up on a farm and have a strong feeling for the land. If I had followed my instincts in the early 60s I would have gotten a landscape degree, but Sea Ranch came along, and I was too busy to pursue it.

JS: This is a totally theory-free question: How do your houses end up being so warm and cozy? I don't know how else to put that.

WT: We make places for people to inhabit, and people inhabit them. If we have done it well, they are going to take over the places and personalize them. If you site the building correctly, it is going to feel like it has been there for awhile. If you put a building in the ground appropriately, and deal with sun and wind, the view, and the existing vegetation, it feels at ease. We probably build closer to trees than most people. You have to snuggle up to the rocks and trees, and if done well, the building seems to be at home. We work with wood when we can afford it. It's a warm material. We are also concerned about light and space; sunlight pours in, and the total ambiance is comfort and warmth. And that equals cozy, even with voluminous spaces.

The greatest challenges for me are non-precedent problems in difficult landscapes, where I can respond to the sense of the place and its cultural past and find a special answer. Then perhaps I can leave something that makes the site seem more memorable for my efforts. That's challenging.

Each job is a problem and an opportunity to solve it. My buildings are not stylish or flashy in a world dominated by advertising, with new models of cars and skirts all the time. Society is conditioned by the print media and the electronic media to respond to change. Different architects have their brief moment in the sun. The media takes a wonderful architect like Frank Gehry, wrings him out, and drops him. And what happens is that young people in school are influenced by the exposure and start doing Gehry better than Gehry, eroding the original to the point where it is tired and predictable, and never learning the lesson. What they are doing is not creative forgetfulness, it is form copying.

JS: How do you communicate those values in a place like the Napa Valley, when the wineries you design are competing for visual attention with enormous wineries designed to be visual extravaganzas? I mean, when I'm up there with nonarchitect friends I point out the fine winery you did for Cakebread and they say. . . .

WT: "Ho-hum. How far to Sterling?" We design buildings to endure in the landscape the way Trefethen has, not to be fashionable billboards with limited appeal.

JS: In a recent issue of *Architecture California* you said that the wineries that fit into the Napa Valley are Robert Pepe, Cakebread, and Johnson Turnbull. And that the ones that don't fit in are ones like Sterling and Clos Pegase.

WT: Yes, but they don't fit in with verve. They are passionate buildings. It's the ones that

lack passion that do not contribute anything. With Sterling or Pegase it doesn't make any difference whether I like them or not, because that is a question of taste. They are built with passion and care.

JS: I mean, though, how do your buildings affect change among nonarchitects? For example, the Napa Valley is becoming one long strip from outside of Napa to above Calistoga. The rural character of the place is in great danger of changing to that of a continual series of roadside attractions.

WT: I do not know. Unless you are a screamer, you are not heard. Two-year-olds know this well. Hopefully, some of the more perceptive people will understand your alternatives. It requires somebody taking the time to stop long enough to consider the situation. If tourists are collecting Kodak images, such as Sterling or the Whitehall Lane winery, they are collecting billboards, and billboard images sell wine as you can notice from their bottle labels.

The theme of your questions is "Why do you do what you do, and of what value is it?" I ask myself the same questions and don't have the final answers. I'm still looking. Each site is different, and each person is different. As an architect, you can wind up in a Saarinan paradox without a stylistically consistent body of work or point of view that can be influential because you are still experimenting. So, the question is, should an architect try to have a more consistent body of work, like Aalto, where there are intellectual clues along the way?

JS: The desire to have the strong imprint of one's own style may be regarded as strong, but may also be seen as a weak or insecure gesture.

WT: I agree with you. My pattern of circling back to the site and landscape is the real strength of my work. I don't know others who use land, landscape, and metaphor to catalyze conceptual answers. It's a method that does not lend itself easily to teaching. So much of it is intuitive, reading the land. I would need to walk a piece of ground with someone to give them a stream-of-consciousness reading of what my eye is seeing and what my mind is working on. I cannot give students a cookbook menu. Each must find his own way, and hopefully, be of use to others. I believe, and worry simultaneously, having matriculated through school under strong instructors, that I have a stewardship obligation to either pass on what I learned or pass on some of my own insights. When we do this the profession operates synergistically and each new generation is not involved in selfish aggrandizement and novel invention for the sake of claiming attention.

Facing page, right: gazebo detail, private residence, Napa Valley.

Right: Civic Center, Mountain View.

Glossary

Aedicula   In contemporary architecture, an open enclosure consisting of supports at four corners and a roof. Based on a small Roman structure, the aedicula became popular in twentieth-century architecture when Louis Kahn introduced it into his work.

American romanticism   Architecture that professes deep roots and connections with the unique spiritual and geographic qualities of America, in contrast to architecture modeled on European ideas and buildings. Architects of this lineage include Frank Lloyd Wright and Bruce Goff.

Axis   A line connecting points in plan and space. In architecture, the line is often a processional path.

Bay regionalism   Architecture in and around San Francisco that claims a strong tie to the locale and its characteristics.

Beaux Arts   In his book, *Classical Architecture/ Rule and Invention*, Thomas Gordon Smith defines Beaux Arts as "the system of architectural education developed in the French Academy in Rome during the eighteenth century and formalized in Paris throughout the nineteenth century." According to Smith, this style of classical architecture was also taught in the United States from the 1890s through the 1930s.

Building envelope   The allowable aboveground volume of a building permitted by planning and building codes.

Butt glazing   Sheets of glass detailed so that separate sheets meet with only a sealant dividing them.

Camber   A slight arching in a beam.

Classicism   Architecture that adheres to the principles and forms of ancient Greek and Roman architecture.

Contextualism   A popular approach within postmodern architecture that calls for designing individual buildings and groups of buildings so that they are woven visually into their surroundings. In his book, *Modern Movements in Architecture*, Charles Jencks describes contextualism as a city-based morphology.

Cornice   The overhang forming the top of an elevation or façade. It originally represented a roof overhang.

Deconstructivism   An approach to architecture in which the architect modifies existing architectural vocabularies, such as late modernist or constructivist vocabularies, through a series of design moves that creates buildings often appearing fragmented, or pulled-apart and rebuilt. For architects working in this manner, deconstructivism emphasizes the metaphysics of alienation; to some observers, the buildings they produce contain, within their own strange beauty, a strongly expressed strain of nihilism.

Demising wall   A wall that divides the adjacent spaces of separately occupied or fire-separated areas in a building.

Drawer job   Reusing the plans of one project, which are stored away in a file drawer, for another.

Eclecticism   A design approach in architecture that draws on elements from many different stylistic and philosophic sources to create a new building.

Floor, cranked   Opposing two or more patterns, structural rhythms, or other architectural elements on a plan so that they exist in an angular, non–right-angle relationship to each other.

Form follows function   A famous architectural dictum attributed to Louis Sullivan meaning that an object acquires its form from its own unique meanings, characteristics, and purpose.

Glu-lam   A wood beam composed of many smaller horizontal strips of wood laminated together.

Header   The beam spanning an opening.

House VI   One of a series of formalist, late modern houses in which Peter Eisenman develops his attitudes about architecture.

International Style   A twentieth-century movement with utopian vision of architecture's ability to transform human lives for the better. It became a codified style characterized by walls articulated as unadorned planes into which openings for windows were cut in strips, flat roofs, and a new expression of structure, often a grid of freestanding columns within a building.

Japanese metabolism   Architecture of the 60s and 70s in Japan that reflected an obsession with how buildings might expand and contract, often modularly, as space requirements change. A forerunner of metabolist architects in Japan was the Archigram group in England.

Loosian   In the manner of Adolph Loos, an early twentieth-century Austrian modern architect. His most famous pronouncement is the terrifying declaration that "ornament is a crime."

Massing   The visual characteristics of an architectural composition with regard to how forms are shaped and opposed to each other and their surroundings.

Midblock alley   In early speculative housing tracts in San Francisco, the alley that divides a city block in half, with residential lots on either side.

Miesian   In the manner of the twentieth-century architect, Mies van der Rohe, who built steel and glass buildings generally articulated in a post and beam vocabulary. His buildings are characterized by a restrained and elegant expression of the steel members.

Minimalism   Restricting the expression and articulation of form, structure, and details in a building. Sometimes minimalist spaces are quite elegant and refined, while others seem anorexic.

Mixed use   Combining uses within one building, such as residential and commercial.

Modernism   An approach to architecture that combines a belief in architecture's power to transform society with a self-conscious break with the past and a search for particularly modern forms and spaces. Modernism believes that new technologies, from the nineteenth-century onward, call for new expressions and allow better lives for humanity.

Neoclassicism   A revival of classical styles, which occurs periodically.

Postmodernism   An approach to architecture that arose in the 60s and 70s as a reaction to modernism. Postmodern buildings may be characterized, as Charles Jencks has written, as appearing to have a "double-coded language." That is, they are modern, because of the technology out of which they are created, but they speak other languages, not based in the contemporary technology of building, chosen by the architects to "communicate with a particular public."

Post-structuralism   A philosophy in the arts and in architecture built on the works of the writer/philosophers Jacques Derrida, Michel Foucault, and Jean Baudrillard. Profoundly skeptical and anticapitalist, it emphasizes what it sees as contemporary alienation, the impossibility of individualism and the inability of modern man to control representation. According to a recent article in *The New Yorker* by Adam Gopnik, copies of Baudrillard's works are kept next to the cash registers in SoHo's bookstores to facilitate purchase.

Punched openings   Window and doors articulated as holes cut into a plane.

Raised podium   An elevated platform on which a building rests.

Rationalism   An architecture that claims to base its design philosophy in the human faculty of reason. Rationalist architecture is characterized by an absence of strongly personal gestures and the use of what rationalists think of as archetypal forms for the building blocks of architecture, such as doors, walls, windows, stairs, and so on. To some, rationalist work is a beautifully restrained architecture juxtaposing simple planes and voids at right angles to each other, while others regard it as a style well suited to building prisons as cheaply as possible.

Reductivism   Reducing spaces, forms, and architectural details to elements which the architect believes have power in their simplicity.

Regionalism   Emphasizing the locale and characteristics of an area in architecture.

Reveal   A pause, or gap, between materials or pieces of a building.

Scale   A relationship of relative size.

Setback   The distance a building must be held back from property lines according to building and planning codes.

Soffit   The underside of a building element. Soffit is often used to describe portions of a modeled ceiling plane or the underside of a beam.

Streamline motif   Dynamic horizontal or diagonal recesses or lines across an architectural surface designed to convey a feeling of movement.

Trellis   A framework of lattice or light structural members, often wood, designed as an overhang or covering to provide a partially shaded pattern or sense of enclosure.

Type 5 one-hour   A type of construction from the Uniform Building Code restricting the area and height of buildings and designating their fire resistances. Type 5 specifies the lowest height among building types according to the code.

Typology   In architecture and urban design, the study, analysis, and classification of buildings and cities by types.

Vernacular   Related to the visual dialect of buildings in an area. Vernacular buildings are in opposition to more universal and formalized ways of designing and building and have not generally been included within the "high culture" of particular societies.